RUFUS CHOATE

Rufus Choate, from a Daguerreotype in the Possession of Charles F. Choate, III, Southboro, Mass.

RUFUS CHOATE

The *Wizard* of the Law

By
CLAUDE M. FUESS

ARCHON BOOKS
1970

Copyright 1928 by Minton, Balch, & Company
Copyright 1956 by Claude M. Fuess
Reprinted 1970
in an unaltered and unabridged edition

ISBN: 0-208-00938-8
Library of Congress Catalog Card Number: 70-114421
[Reproduced from a copy in the Yale University Library]
Printed in the United States of America

CONTENTS

ILLUSTRATIONS

RUFUS CHOATE

Rufus Choate

CHAPTER I

The Background

He must be indeed an unreasonable creature who, having America
for a continent and Massachusetts for a state and Essex for a county
is not entirely satisfied.—*Joseph H. Choate.*

*N*ATIVES of Essex County, on the Massachusetts
seaboard, have always maintained that it has unusual
scenic variety and charm. From the New Hampshire
border at Salisbury its coast stretches south to the wide
Merrimac sweeping over the shallows at Newburyport,
where one can still see what Whittier described as

> The sand-bluffs at the river's mouth,
> The swinging chain-bridge, and, afar,
> The foam-line of the harbor bar.

Along the weird drumlins, gravel banks, and glacial
bowlders of Plum Island the shore line runs, to the
heights of Castle Neck and the spits and stratified ridges
of Ipswich, where the wind-driven sand encroaches upon

[3]

farmlands and orchards; around the "gray rocks of Cape Ann" and the beacon at Eastern Point to Gloucester Harbor, with its fishing vessels; then, somewhat southwest, past Singing Beach and Beverly and a score of wooded islands to picturesque old Salem and the toy peninsulas of Marblehead and Nahant; and finally into the placid bay at Lynn. In the interior, back only a few miles from the ocean, are the rolling hills of Hamilton and Wenham and the forests of Boxford, where unsuspected lakes are hidden among the hollows, with fragrant pines on the enclasping knolls. Still farther to the west are Lawrence and Haverhill, the crowded cosmopolitan cities on the Merrimac, and beautiful Andover, on the Shawsheen, with its graceful towers rising above the brick of its ancient school.

There was a time when the maritime commerce of Essex County, meager enough to-day, was the basis of Massachusetts prosperity. In 1790 the most populous towns of the Commonwealth, excluding Boston, were Salem, Newburyport, Marblehead, and Gloucester,— all Essex County ports. Fortunes were made in the late eighteenth century by those who followed the sea. Along the wharves the passer-by could scent the pleasing odors of tar and salt spray, mingled with the vague fragrance of spices from the Indies. Hulls were laid down and launched along the Merrimac, sometimes a score in a single season. The sailors lurching from the inn doors might be just back from Havana or Calcutta or Zanzibar with cargoes of molasses or silks or ivory. Read a story like Hergesheimer's *Java Head* to catch the spirit of Salem in those "spacious days." The avenues of Newburyport and its rival towns were being lined with square brick mansions, substantial symbols of the wealth amassed in foreign trade. It was a period of ceaseless activity, when no enterprise was too hazardous and no risk too doubtful.

This intense vitality inevitably produced virile men; and Essex County, although comprising only some five hundred square miles of not very fertile soil, became, like Athens and Florence in their prime, conspicuous for its leaders. It was settled by a fine class of immigrants, whose descendants had the advantage of good blood. Of merchant princes there were many, like the Silsbees and Derbys and Crowninshields and Pickmans from Salem and the Tracys, Jacksons, Hoopers, and Cushings from Newburyport. William Gray and Stephen Higginson made the opulence of Salem rival that of Nineveh and Tyre. But money-getting was not all. From Newburyport emerged Senator Tristram Dalton and Chief Justice Theophilus Parsons and Judge John Lowell and Caleb Cushing and William Lloyd Garrison. There Rufus King and Robert Treat Paine and John Quincy

Adams, as gay young blades, studied law in the midst of a sophisticated society which Adams has vividly described. There too dwelt that inebriated and eccentric philosopher, Lord Timothy Dexter, whose gilded eagle still poises gayly above his former home on High Street and whose whimsicalities have been the delight of his biographers. From Salem came Timothy Pickering, John Adams's austere and uncompromising Secretary of State, the embodiment of New England Federalism at its best and worst; Nathaniel Hawthorne, the "rebellious Puritan," who so subtly portrayed the evanescent melancholy of colonial times; and Robert Rantoul, Jr., the aristocrat who espoused the cause of the people. In Andover there were Samuel Osgood, first Postmaster General of the United States, and a long array of Phillipses, founders and benefactors of important schools. From Amesbury came the true interpreter of the New England countryside, John Greenleaf Whittier, the poet of "Old Floyd Ireson" and "The Witch of Wenham" and "The Garrison of Cape Ann," who wrote of Essex County as a lover writes of his sweetheart. And from Hog Island, in Chebacco, appeared Rufus Choate, the strangest, the least explicable, and, with the exception of Hawthorne, the rarest spirit of them all.

Near the mouths of the Castle Neck and Ipswich Rivers, removed in places only a few yards from the low marshy shore of the mainland, is Hog Island, thus rudely named because its long sloping ridge resembles a pig's back. Motorists along the highway from Ipswich to Gloucester see it for miles as one of the most conspicuous features of the landscape. It lies in a kind of a harbor, almost shut off from the wide Atlantic by the promontories of Castle Neck and Coffin's Beach. Sensitive modern souls have renamed the spot "Choate's Island," and have written verses about it:

> Half from the marshy fen, half from the tide,
> In front Choate Island rises steep and bold;
> Its treeless summit and its rocky side
> Against that northern sky show bleak and bold.

To natives of the district, however, it has always been Hog Island, and Hog Island it will probably remain.

Residents of Essex County often travel thousands of miles, to Cornwall or the French Riviera, to rhapsodize over vistas no finer than that which lies within walking distance of their homes. As one stands on the shore near Castle Neck, he sees in the foreground the white sand dunes, gleaming like hammered silver against the changing azure of the waves beyond. Never the same from hour to hour, these rounded heaps are always fascinating, whether their tiny particles are being scattered about by the December winds or lie, motionless and bak-

[7]

ing, like a portion of the Sahara, in the glare of an August sun. Farther on lie the marshes, surrounded by mud-flats if the tide happens to be low. Back of these, slowly rising from the water, emerges the island itself, like some gigantic leviathan of the voyager's imagination; and in the dim distance are visible, as a background, the ledges of Annisquam and Cape Ann. It is a spectacle which Rufus Choate, from his childhood to his old age, always surveyed with satisfaction in his soul.

The three hundred acres of the island are first mentioned in history as an Indian burying-ground, a sacred place to the red men. After the coming of the white settlers, it was sold to the town of Ipswich and finally divided among the citizens, each receiving a lot of three and one-half acres. A certain John Choate, who had joined the Chebacco Parish in 1643, gradually bought up the shares of his neighbors until he owned them all; and his third son, Thomas, with his girl bride, Mary Varney, started housekeeping there in 1690, as the earliest white residents of the island. It was natural that Thomas should be known as "Governor" Choate, for the entire island was soon transferred to him by his father, and he became its sole proprietor.

Hog Island, although now deserted except for summer visitors, is nevertheless a princely domain. As the descendants of "Governor" Choate multiplied,—and there was no danger of race suicide among them,—three separate farms were laid out, and, from 1691 to 1805, eighty babies of the Choate name were born there, the children of eleven different families. Their daily lives could not have been precisely sybaritic. There are periods, of course, when the continent at low tide seems only a stone's throw away; indeed an audacious Jacob Choate, in 1751, as a child of five, acquired prestige by riding horseback from the island to the head of the creek and back again, the path being always under water. But in the winter the Choate farms must have been shut off from civilization for days at a stretch. The legend has been handed down of Hannah Choate, who woke on her wedding day in January, 1793, to find that the heavy tide and floating ice made it impossible for the bridegroom to row over from Ipswich. Patiently she sat down at her foot-wheel to spin and worked zealously until evening. Then the storm subsided, the wedding party crossed without capsizing, and the knot was tied by Parson Cleaveland.

In our less primitive times, men and women have not been willing to endure such separation from their kind; consequently the three old farmhouses have long been unoccupied. But there was no lack of occupation or of companionship on Hog Island in the eighteenth century. At one period it boasted sixteen marriageable Choate

[9]

girls, all "exceeding fair," who were carried off one by one by farmer boys from Ipswich township. A grizzled patriarch who had seen his seventh daughter wedded and taken away, cried, "I do believe they'll come for my wife next!" All through the century there was a small self-contained community on Hog Island. A Choate was born there as late as 1802, and Rufus Choate himself was the last child on the original farm of the "Governor." Because of some family superstition, the bodies of the dead were invariably buried in a cemetery on the mainland.

The descendants of Thomas Choate were a tough-fibered, uncomplaining, and independent clan. Their assurance is illustrated by the story of William Choate, a mariner, who was summoned as a witness in an English court, presided over by Lord Ellenborough. To the inquiries of the magistrate, William replied simply, "Yes, sir" or "No, sir," instead of "Yes, my lord" and "No, my lord." A barrister turned angrily to him and asked, "What country were you born in that you presume to answer his lordship 'Yes, sir' and 'No, sir'?" The native of Hog Island, six feet tall and weighing nearly two hundred pounds, stared back at the attorney and, in a voice as clear as a silver trumpet, responded, "I was born in a country where there is but one Lord, and that is the Lord in the Heavens!"

Inured to hardships and discomforts, the Choates became a shrewd and practical race, blest with common-sense and quick to adapt themselves to emergencies. Physically they were rugged and powerful, living long lives except when they were cut short by accident. Seven of them at least were Revolutionary veterans, two of them dying of disease while in the army. One was captured by a privateer in 1812 and was confined for three years in Dartmoor Prison. Some of them, driven by restlessness, became pioneers in undeveloped sections of the country,—in the backwoods of Maine, in the Northwest Territory, and even beyond the Mississippi. One of them, Leander Choate, moved from Massachusetts to Oshkosh, Wisconsin, and became President of a Log and Lumber Company, a banker and business man far from Hog Island. His square, rugged, Yankee face, the lower jaw fringed with a beard, is devoid of romanticism. He seems in his photographs to be the very embodiment of practicality,—a kind of Middle Western David Harum.

The stay-at-home Choates on Hog Island did not become millionaires nor did they raise great mansions, like the Tracys and the Jacksons. They were simple, unpretentious people, uncorrupted by luxurious living. Of the Choate sons, a large proportion followed the sea for a livelihood, as sailors, officers, and owners of ships.

It was a time when a youngster of spirit turned instinctively to the ocean and what it had to offer for excitement. Rufus's grandfather, William, was captain of a ship at twenty-five, and his four sons were all taught the art of navigation. In the family annals we find repeated again and again the tragic phrases "drowned" or "lost at sea." In 1784, two boats with nine men rowing ashore from a fishing vessel were upset and eight of the sailors were drowned, including Ephraim Choate and his son. In 1804, John Choate was struck by lightning on board a ship and instantly killed. In 1817, two of Rufus's cousins were drowned in a West Indies hurricane while on board the *Caesar*. There was always danger for those who went down to the sea in ships. It is significant that the births of children on Hog Island were recorded as taking place at high or low tide. Rufus Choate was born to the music of breakers dashing upon the shore.

They were of sound and unblemished stock, these Choates of Hog Island. Among them there were no rogues or desperadoes, but honest, god-fearing people, whose living was as plain as their thinking was high. There were many of them in Chebacco,—so many that it was said that you could not throw a stone anywhere without hitting a Choate or a Burnham. Not all of them were successful as the world measures achievement, but most of them were respected in their own communities. Among the more than two thousand direct descendants of John Choate, there have been many farmers, and mariners, but also teachers, clergymen, lawyers, judges, bankers, and statesmen, several of whom, like Rufus Choate and Joseph Hodges Choate and Charles F. Choate, Jr., the Boston lawyer who died only a short time ago, have been men of unusual talent. This is a remarkable record for any family. I have studied their faces in the Choate *Genealogy*, and they are countenances to be trusted.

Among them all, however, there has been no other like Rufus! His wrinkled and furrowed cheeks, his shaggy brush of hair, and the unfathomed pathos of his eyes set him apart from his brothers and cousins. Compared with them, he was like a peacock among domestic fowl or a gorgeous orchid in a garden of commonplace daffodils and dahlias. Joseph H. Choate, his distant relative, described him as a "mercurial child of the sun," and marveled that he should have been nurtured under the chilling blasts of our New England east winds. On what perverse principle of heredity came this romantic personality into the nursery of the practical Choates? Here and there it is possible to point to a Choate who had some one of Rufus's characteristics,—his industry, his passion for accuracy, his legal acumen, or his love

[13]

of the sea. Even his oratorical gifts may possibly be paralleled in those of Colonel Benjamin Choate of stentorian voice, who, according to tradition, could be heard from East Hill in Enfield, New Hampshire, giving the word of command to his regiment at Canaan Street five miles down the valley. But in his combination of qualities Rufus was unique. How could he have been born on Hog Island, in Essex County, Commonwealth of Massachusetts? A more fitting cradle would have been Penang or Rangoon or some minareted city of the Orient.

Rufus's grandfather, William Choate, was first a sailor, owning and commanding vessels, and then a teacher. He was "the handsomest man on the island, tall, with black hair and dark complexion." He and his wife, Mary Giddings, had ten children, of whom David, Rufus's father, was the oldest to survive infancy. This David was less rugged than most of the Choates, and his Diary is full of references to his ailments. When he reached twenty-one, in 1778, he became a teacher, like his father, and was regarded as a youth of unusual intelligence. In the spring of 1780, he, with six others, two of whom were Choates, walked from Chebacco to West Point, where they joined a regiment in Lafayette's Infantry; but he fought in no engagements. After the war, he spent eighteen months on a voyage which carried him to Cuba and Spain. It was his education, for there was no money to send him and his brothers to college.

At twenty-seven, having seen something of the world, David married "Polly" Cogswell, who, however, died within two months after the wedding. The death of his father in 1785 left him with a small property, and he settled down as a farmer on the mainland. Then, in 1791, he took as a wife Miriam Foster, daughter of Captain Aaron and Ruth Foster, of Chebacco. She has been described as "a quiet, sedate, but cheerful woman, dignified in manner, quick in perception, of strong sense and ready wit," but these commonplace phrases tell us little of what she really was. In the following spring he moved with her to Hog Island, into the farmhouse which had been built about 1725 by his grandfather, Francis Choate. It is perched on the easterly side of the island, facing the open sea,—an unadorned and charmless habitation, with a central chimney, two full stories, and a high gabled roof. One of the family has pictured it in verse:

> Upon this slope the ancient farmhouse stands,
> Its beams and rafters true in every line,
> Built for the centuries with honest hands
> In Puritanic plainness of design.

Here children were born to Miriam and David,— two daughters, Mary and Hannah; a son, David, named after his father; and then Rufus, who entered this world, on the testimony of the family Bible, "Tuesday, Oct. 1, 1799, at 3 o'clock, P. M." Somebody must have employed ingenuity at his christening, for there was no Rufus in any close branch of the family. The name, however, was not very appropriate, for it means "red," and the boy grew up with hair as black as the raven's. He was born in the front corner chamber, on the left of the front door. The pine cradle in which he, like so many infant Choates before him, was rocked, was long preserved in the room of his birth. It was taken to the Philadelphia Centennial Exposition and shown in the collection of antiquities, and it is now in the attic of the Choate homestead at Essex. Modern science does not approve of rocking babies, and it will doubtless never again be used for that purpose.

In the April following Rufus's birth, David moved back to the mainland, where he purchased a house on Spring Street, in Chebacco, recently left vacant by the death of Parson John Cleaveland. Tearing down the disintegrating structure, David built himself a new home, which still stands, somewhat remodeled, and is in the possession of direct descendants of David Choate. From the upper windows, little Rufus could look out

The House on Hog Island in which Rufus Choate was Born

in a northeasterly direction towards Hog Island and the marshes which lie near it, and it was only a short stroll to salt water. Here David dwelt until his death in 1808.

Edwin P. Whipple, observing Rufus Choate later in Salem, noted that there seemed to be no connection between the man and his environment. It was a case in which all the laws of inheritance were disproved. It should be possible for a biologist to discover in Choate's ancestors hints of the tendencies which he displayed; but it cannot be done. David Choate was trusted by his associates, and, if his health had not failed, might have revealed qualities of leadership. Both parents were pleasant sagacious people, with a taste for reading. But no seer could have predicted that, from their union, or from the Choate family of Hog Island, would emerge the strange phenomenon of Rufus Choate, bringing with him a suggestion of boundless and inexplicable mystery.

CHAPTER II

The Formative Years

*T*HE Chebacco Parish in which Rufus Choate grew up separated in 1819 from Ipswich and became the town of Essex. The very center of Essex village lies on the main thoroughfare between Ipswich and Gloucester and is traversed to-day during the summer by long lines of motor cars going to and from the North Shore resorts. Billboards and restaurant signs mar the attractiveness of the landscape, and a flaring gasoline station occupies the corner of Spring Street, only a few rods from the peaceful and secluded house where Choate spent his boyhood.

A few half-completed hulls on the ways near the river are reminiscent of the past, and the sight of Hog Island encourages us with the thought that some aspects of Nature cannot be entirely mutilated by man; but the old quaint charm of Essex is gone. The village has been changed to meet the demands of our feverish modern life.

For the moment, however, we must let imagination

take us back to the early nineteenth century, when Rufus Choate was a lad and Chebacco was a sleepy fishing hamlet, from which forty sail went out for cod and mackerel and where a score or more of small vessels were launched between May and November. The population of barely eleven hundred was scattered over an area of about twenty square miles, of which a considerable portion was marshland or water. It is difficult for us to comprehend a society in which candles took the place of electric lights, and drinking water was drawn laboriously from wells; in which a bath was a ceremony instead of a mere incident in daily routine; in which Sunday was a day of rest and meditation, interrupted only by church services; in which a trip to Ipswich or Gloucester was a matter of hours instead of minutes, and not to be undertaken lightly; in which open fires and stoves supplied all the warmth through the frigid New England winter; in which countless people died because of lack of medical knowledge and incompetent nursing; in which railroads and steamboats, —to say nothing of automobiles, radios, moving pictures, and airplanes,—would have seemed as miraculous as the resurrection of Lazarus from the dead. It was, from our sophisticated point of view, not a comfortable period; but it did stress some of the simple, almost forgotten virtues, and it developed strength of character

[19]

in those who were fortunate enough to survive its hardships.

In the new house on Spring Street, the Choate family spent their winters, but each summer they moved to the farm on Hog Island. In either case, the boy looked out on "a landscape of austere beauty, with its monotonous, far-reaching meadows and weather-beaten hills." The sea was never far off. To swim and to sail a boat were to him as natural as to breathe. As a child hardly out of kilts, Rufus felt the stinging salt spray against his cheeks as he paddled down the river in his home-made dugout, through the long marsh grasses and across the narrow channel to his island home. During the struggle for naval supremacy between England and the United States, he heard tales of battles and was stirred to anger as he was told of the outrage of the *Leopard* upon the *Chesapeake*. When the War of 1812, so unpopular in Massachusetts, was imminent, he played at sea-fights with his companions. His grandmother Choate told him the story of how, during the Revolution, when a British frigate was seen in the bay and twelve men were stationed on Hog Island to prevent boats from landing, the guard fled, and she was left alone with her two children, declaring that she would stay and keep the house even if the soldiers ran. Once Rufus caught a glimpse of the *Tenedos* and the *Shannon*, British men-of-war, "sitting like two swans upon the water of the harbor." From his surroundings in those early days he received enduring impressions, revealed later in the wealth of imagery which he drew from wind and waves, and in the intensity and constancy with which he loved the ocean. Like many Choates before him, he dreamed of commanding a vessel, and the sight of spreading sails filled him with exultation.

Anybody brought up on the Massachusetts coast is familiarized with all varieties of weather and with every wind in the bag of Aeolus. Long after he had left Essex County, Rufus Choate did not forget the experiences of his youth, and, in a speech in the Senate in 1844, he said:

Take the New England climate in summer; you would think the world was coming to an end. . . . Cold to-day, hot to-morrow; mercury at eighty degrees in the morning, with a wind at southwest, and in three hours more a sea-turn, wind at east, a thick fog from the very bottom of the ocean, and a fall of forty degrees Fahrenheit; now so dry as to kill all the beans in New Hampshire, then floods carrying off the bridges and dams of the Penobscot and the Connecticut; snow in Portsmouth in July, and the next day a man and a yoke of oxen killed by lightning in Rhode Island,—you would think the world was twenty times coming to an end! But I don't know how it is; we go along; the early and the later rain falls each in his season; seed time and harvest do not fail; the sixty days of hot corn weather are pretty sure to be measured out to us; the Indian summer with its bland southwest wind and mitigated sunshine brings all up; and on the twenty-fifth of November, or thereabouts, being Thursday, three millions of grateful people, in meeting-houses, or around the family board, give thanks for a year of health, plenty, and happiness.

And yet, in spite of this grimly humorous description, Choate had, all through his life, a longing for the "sun of Essex." He was not a true Nature lover. He had nothing of the passion for flowers and trees and all living things which so dominated the moods of a man like Thoreau. But he did, in his mature and heavily burdened years, frequently find solace in returning to the scenes of his boyhood, where he could contemplate the vast expanse of sky and sea.

It was, however, books, not Nature, that became the controlling force in Rufus Choate's life. David Choate had most of the standard classics,—Milton, Addison, and Johnson, as well as Shakspere. Before he was six years old, Rufus had devoured *Pilgrim's Progress,*— the great adventure story of Puritan New England. Around the Choate hearthstone the Bible was read aloud daily, the Old Testament and the New Testament being covered every two years. Hearing it thus evening after evening, he learned most of the psalms by heart, and he could recite long passages from the prophets. As a child, he was steeped in its archaic phraseology; and his speeches are adorned with Biblical quotations. "I would have the Bible read," he declared, "not only for its authoritative revelations, and its commands and exactions, obligatory yesterday, to-day, and forever, but for its English, for its literature, for its dim imagery, its sayings of consolation and wisdom and universal truth." The *Westminster Catechism* also he memorized at his mother's knee and recited every Sunday before church.

There appears upon this earth now and then a genuine bibliophile, for whom most of life is encompassed within the pages of printed volumes. Such a phenomenon was Rufus Choate. It was not merely religious treatises that he enjoyed. His taste was eclectic. He read while he walked. He read while he ate his meals. He could not go on a trip of four days to the White Mountains without a trunk full of books. His conception of perfect bliss was leisure in a vast library, and he himself accumulated more than eight thousand volumes. Whenever he could snatch a moment from his professional engagements, he seized a book in his hands. Once he was invited by a friend, Charles G. Loring, to spend a day at the latter's estate at Beverly, one of the beauty spots along the North Shore. Choate apparently was pleased with the scenery of forest and ocean, but, when he left at night to return to Boston, he said with rare candor, "My dear Loring, there has not been a twentieth part of a minute since I entered this terrestrial paradise that I have not enjoyed to the top of my bent; but let me tell you that should you confine me here for a week apart from my work and my books, I know that I should die from utter *ennui*. You are fortunate in being able serenely to delight in it day after day." He confessed on another occasion that, if he were to go to Newport for a vacation without his books, he should hang himself before evening.

Choate's thirst for knowledge was insatiable. It was an overwhelming desire, which dominated all his waking hours. With startling precocity he raced through the shelves of the Chebacco "social library," with its nearly four hundred volumes, absorbed at one moment in Rollin's *Ancient History*, at another in Plutarch's *Lives*, grasping avidly at biography, philosophy, poetry, anything which met his eye, and always remembering what he had read. When Choate and Webster were at dinner at the home of James W. Paige, in Boston, they fell to talking about the custom, prevalent enough in their youth, of learning poetry by heart. Webster quoted one of Watts's hymns; Choate capped it with another; and so they kept on for more than an hour, while the other guests encouraged them with applause.

Before Rufus was nine years old, his invalid father

died, and Miriam Choate was left with a family of five small children, the sixth, and youngest,—Job,—having been buried just two weeks before the father. Her grief at thus losing with terrifying swiftness both her son and her husband must have been overwhelming, but she had no time to nurse her sorrow. Hungry mouths had to be fed, and she was the only one to do it.

If she had not been obliged to count her pennies so carefully, Miriam Choate might have tried to give her two older boys a year at a school like Phillips Academy, Andover, only a few miles away. With conditions as they were, she had to be satisfied with the initiation into Latin which David and Rufus received under Dr. Thomas Sewall, a Chebacco physician, who was then boarding in the Choate household and had plenty of time both to guide the lads in their grammar and to woo their oldest sister, Mary, whom he afterwards married. In the summer of 1810, they were permitted to attend a small private school opened by the Reverend Thomas Holt, a young Yale man who had recently been installed as minister of the parish. Later Rufus was sent to a succession of different schools, first under William Cogswell, and then under Center Merrill, Samuel Sewall, John Rogers, and Robert Crowell, the last named being another local clergyman, who married the second Choate daughter, Hannah.

[25]

David, three years older than Rufus, was a delicate and sensitive lad, quick at his studies but poorly equipped physically for a farmer's life; accordingly the family exchequer was stretched to allow him a term at Atkinson Academy, in New Hampshire. At nineteen, when many callow youths are to-day just entering college, David Choate was a teacher in district schools, no longer financially a burden on his mother and actually able to contribute to her support. Recognizing Rufus's brilliance, he resolved to sacrifice his own future in order that his brother might have his chance. Sheer economic pressure had driven Choate boys for four generations out into life without the advantage of a college training. David, who had advanced just far enough to perceive the value of an education, could not help seeing that Rufus was evidently designed by destiny for scholastic triumphs. It was David, then, who, with extraordinary fraternal self-effacement, made it possible for Rufus to go to Dartmouth College.

Somehow money was provided to send Rufus to a now forgotten academy in Hampton, New Hampshire, which he entered in January, 1815. There he spent seven months, patiently reviewing his studies under Preceptor James Adams and trying to fill the gaps in his previous rather desultory preparation. When he left in July, he bore with him a letter of recommendation in which Adams declared that his pupil had read under his surveillance Virgil's *Aeneid*, Cicero's *Orations*, and the Greek *Testament*. "I think," added Master Adams, "that he has studied them thoroughly." Although only two members of his class at Dartmouth were younger than he, Rufus Choate, at sixteen, was not exceptionally precocious as compared, for instance, with Caleb Cushing and George Bancroft, who both graduated from Harvard at seventeen, or with Edward Everett, who, at nineteen, was Pastor of the Church in Brattle Square, in Boston.

In August, 1815, Rufus Choate left his Chebacco home and traveled northwest and inland to the small college on the upper Connecticut. How he reached there is not certain. Often in those days ambitious boys walked scores of miles to secure an education; but Rufus probably had money enough to enable him to ride by coach and stage over the "Fourth Turnpike," through Derry and Concord, Boscawen and Andover, to shaded Lebanon and the village of Hanover, in a country quite unlike that to which he had been accustomed in Essex County. He was now near the mountains, with Ascutney close by and taller peaks visible in the distance on cloudless days.

Rufus Choate was an undergraduate at Dartmouth during the four most critical years of its history, when the Dartmouth College Controversy was at its height. Although some of the ramifications of this contest are difficult to follow, authorities agree that it was basically the result of an effort of the Democratic New Hampshire Legislature to gain control of the institution. At Commencement in August, 1815, just before Choate matriculated, the self-perpetuating and conservative Board of Trustees, functioning under a royal charter granted in 1769, removed Dr. John Wheelock from the Presidency, which he had held for thirty-six years, and elected in his place the Reverend Francis Brown. In the following April, the Democratic Legislature, urged on by Governor Plumer, passed a measure incorporating a new institution to be called Dartmouth University, transferring to it all the buildings and revenues of Dartmouth College, and creating a Board of Overseers, to be appointed by the Governor and Council. The effect was to transform the college into a state institution and thus to make it a political shuttlecock. The Federalist Trustees naturally resented this drastic action, refused to give way, and brought suit before the Superior Court of New Hampshire to recover the records and seal of the College. The suit at once raised the question of the constitutionality of the legislative act establishing the University, and the case was fought through the courts until it finally reached the Supreme Court of the

United States. While the decisions were pending, the newly created University, although it was never fully organized, had legal control over Dartmouth Hall and the other collegiate property, with the result that lectures and recitations had to be held wherever adequate space could be procured. Confusion often prevailed, and the rival factions had some open quarrels, especially when two separate catalogues appeared in the same week. Nothing but the unswerving loyalty of both instructors and students kept the machinery in operation during that time of uncertainty, when nobody could be quite sure from month to month whether the College would survive.

In Choate's period, there were fewer than 150 in the student body, and the graduating classes rarely numbered more than forty. There were only five teachers besides the President, and the facilities for work, even before the controversy began, were decidedly limited. Yet it was in those primitive days, when funds were not plentiful and the enrollment was small, that the college graduated its two most famous alumni,—Daniel Webster and Rufus Choate. Webster, who had been a member of the class of 1801, had become, by 1815, a power in Congress and a lawyer of more than local reputation. The Dartmouth of the twentieth century, with its huge gymnasium and stadium, its noble Daniel

Webster Hall, its beautiful new library, and its impressive physical equipment, has not yet produced a Webster or a Choate.

Throughout his course Choate lived in boarding houses,—during the last two years at the home of the scholarly Professor Ebenezer Adams. His bills for tuition, fines, and other charges during four years amounted to $97.73, and, when he took his degree, the college generously allowed him to give his promissory note for the balance due,—$84.14. Probably he felt that he was receiving his money's worth, for he made the most of his opportunities. After his arrival in Hanover, he was ordered to appear before several members of the faculty in turn, to be tested in Greek, Latin, English, and Arithmetic. For the first term of his Freshman year he did not shine. Some better trained youths from Phillips Academy, Andover, went ahead of him with a running start. But it was not long before the diffident lad, with his fresh, ruddy complexion and sparkling eager eyes, showed that he had the spirit of the true scholar, and his native gifts of memory and concentration soon enabled him to pass others who had originally a better foundation.

During the Winter Term, only ten or twelve of Choate's thirty-three classmates remained in Hanover, the others having taken positions as teachers in schools in order to earn money. "How thankful I ought to be," he wrote, "that I am not *obliged* to resort to this for assistance. We who remain have a chance to improve in the languages particularly." Choate spent this precious time very profitably. "In college," he told Parker, "I never went to bed before one o'clock, and then rose very early to prayers, without then feeling it." While his friends were fast asleep, Choate sat at his pine table, the candle throwing a dim light on his book, his head resting on his palms, his elbows propped up in front of him, and his slender fingers running now and then through his disordered hair. His mind worked with startling rapidity, and he soon left slower intellects far in the rear. When he had reached Sophomoric dignity, he had acquired sufficient confidence to lay out for himself a course of study which included much more than the prescribed Cicero, Greek, Geography, Algebra, Geometry, and Logic. It was admitted of him that, in the field of scholarship, "no one pretended to rival him nor did he invite comparison." Even then he had learned a lesson which he later shared with others,—"Desultory reading is a waste of life. Read by system."

The current conception of college as a glorified country club, devoted largely to social festivities and athletic contests, would not have appealed to Rufus Choate. He was quite serious when he spoke of "the friendship of scholars, growing out of a unanimity of high and honorable pursuits." He viewed Dartmouth as a place where one acquired wisdom and understanding, and he considered "extra-curriculum activities" as inconsistent with his aims. It is not strange that, holding this opinion, he was soon the acknowledged leader of his class, maintaining that position until graduation, but wearing all his academic honors with such modesty that envy of him was banished by admiration of his talents.

From month to month, in the fashion of that day, he was steeping himself in classical literature. From his tenth to his twentieth years he followed an almost uninterrupted course in Latin and Greek, subjects which then provided an intensive training such as nothing else could offer. In middle age, Choate said:

My college life was so exquisitely happy that I should like to relive it in my son. The studies of Latin and Greek,—Livy, Horace, Tacitus, Xenophon, Herodotus, and Thucydides,—had ever a charm beyond expression, and the first opening of our great English authors, Milton, Addison, Johnson, and the great writers for the reviews, made that time of my life a brief sweet dream. They created tastes and supplied sources of enjoyment which support me to this day.

It is pleasant to hear from one of Choate's friendly rivals how he put Livy's Latin into "exquisitely fit and sweet English. . . in comparison with which all the other construing of the morning seemed the roughest of unlicked babble." To the close of his career, Choate delighted in the ancient masterpieces, reading in them daily, bringing quotations from them into his speeches, and turning to them for solace in weary hours. As a Congressman in Washington, at the age of forty-four, he wrote in his *Journal*:

I was able to-day almost to resume my courses, such as they are, of classical and elegant reading,—Johnson's *Life of Addison*, the *Odyssey*, Thucydides, Tacitus, Juvenal, Horace's *Art of Poetry* in Dancier and Hurd.

Choate early displayed an aptitude for platform speaking. There was some required declamation in the Dartmouth curriculum, and the "Wednesday Rhetoricals" were an established although not always a popular feature of the week's program. The boys composed their own speeches, but "tragedies, plays, and all irreligious expressions and sentiments" were "sacredly prohibited." Choate was arbitrarily assigned to membership in the "Social Friends," one of the two rival debating societies, and took a leading part in its exercises. He was a student before he went to Dartmouth, but Dartmouth made him an orator,—or rather provided him with the facilities for proving and developing his native talent. For a time he was Librarian of the Social Friends, and, in 1817, when some officers of the phantom University tried to assert their legal rights by attempting to carry off by force the books belonging to the two literary societies, Choate, with some others, put up an effective resistance, as a consequence of which he was arrested on a charge of "riot" and bound over to the Grand Jury; but the circumstances were such that no bill was found against the defendants. It was Rufus Choate's first experience with the law in its practical operation.

When, at the opening of his Senior year, Choate was elected President of the Social Friends, he made a brilliant address at the initiation of the new members from the Freshman Class. Long after the event, several of those present could recall distinctly what the young orator had to say regarding those elements of character essential to the ripe scholar and the useful citizen. When he declaimed, "Our learned men are the hope and strength of the nation," he was propounding a doctrine which he was to reiterate in his later lectures. Choate's power as an orator even then was shown not merely through his tone modulations and gestures, but through the richness of his style and the firmness and clarity of his thought. One of those who frequently heard him confessed that Choate's declamatory exercises

[34]

in Dartmouth gave him "an absorbing and rapt sensation of delight." He left behind him in Hanover memories of the contagious fervor of his manner and the fascination of his eye and voice.

What were his recreations? Then, as later, his chief diversion was in a change of work. He cared nothing for outdoor sports, although he occasionally stretched his muscles on a tramp over the hills around Hanover with his friend Tenney, a jovial, light-hearted youth, temperamentally the antipodes of Choate. Fraternities were as yet unknown in Dartmouth, but Choate did enjoy relaxation with his fellows, and his room has been described as a center of mirth and wit. He did not, however, indulge in even the milder forms of undergraduate frivolity and dissipation. His preferred source of relaxation was books,—and then more books!

It is not surprising that, in the end, he broke down nervously. As early as the close of his Freshman year, he wrote his brother, "Should I have my health, my acquirements ought to be great. . . . I feel rather unwell, but a few days will decide." As a Sophomore, he confided to his family, "I have too much neglected exercise, and my head suffers for it. Since conversing with Dr. Mussey, I have altered my habits and regularly exercise every day." These headaches, apparently neuralgic in character, became so frequent and so severe as to interfere with his attendance at lectures. Finally, as a Senior, he had a really serious illness, probably a form of neurasthenia. He lost flesh; he became so feeble that he could hardly walk across the Common; and his ghastly pallor was heartrending to his companions. Dr. Mussey, the Hanover physician, took him into his own household, hoping to build up his strength by attention to rest and diet, but he did not improve. When the Commencement appointments were announced, Choate, despite his many absences, was named as Valedictorian, but it was feared that he would not be able to appear at the closing ceremonies.

On the morning of the great day in 1819 there was doubt as to whether Choate could face the ordeal, and it was even whispered that he was too weak to rise from his bed. The procession of dignitaries was formed without him, and the exercises began with his seat vacant. The College Church, with its glistening white pews and its low gallery on three sides, was packed with people, all wondering what would happen. When the Valedictory was called for, however, Rufus Choate appeared from a side entrance and moved with languid step to the platform, as if the mere struggle to lift one foot from the floor were too enervating. . . . It was the first of many such dramatic moments in Choate's career. He had doubtless read in history of that occasion when the

Earl of Chatham was borne into the House of Lords, swathed in flannels, to speak on the rights of the American colonies, and of that other memorable day when Fisher Ames, believing that his end was near, had held the United States Senate spellbound, in 1796, on the subject of Jay's Treaty. On a smaller scale, this was a similar situation; and Rufus Choate, like the consummate actor that he was, knew how to make the most of its possibilities.

Emaciated and tremulous, with colorless cheeks, deep-sunk and glowing eyes, and hair in disorder above his somber gown, he was an apparition like those which tortured Macbeth. Saluting the Trustees and officers of the college, he opened his remarks in a low quavering voice, which the rear seats had to strain to hear. But when he turned to say "Good-bye!" to his classmates on the benches behind him, he seemed to gather himself for one supreme effort as if he had been reserving his last ounce of strength until it was needed. It was a farewell which he considered to be final, for he had been warned that he had not long to live:

Go, go forward, my classmates, with all your honors and all your hopes. You will leave me behind, lingering or cut short on the way; but I shall carry to my grave, however, wherever, whenever, I shall be called hence, the delightful remembrance of our joys and our love.

[37]

In this Valedictory Address, Choate revealed the intense earnestness, and many of the peculiar mannerisms, which were to distinguish his later platform successes. That he was a natural orator, intuitively the master of the technique of his art, was obvious to all who heard him on that Commencement morning. By studied self-discipline, he made progress as the years went on; but in Dartmouth he was already a great public speaker. . . . The effect was all that Choate could have desired. There is a tradition that a rustic maiden from Norwich, Vermont, listened and wept, and, on the following Monday, while bending over the washtub, sobbed, "Mother, you can't think how pretty that young man who had the valedictory spoke. He was so interesting that I cried, and I can't help crying now, only thinking of it!" Even the more sophisticated among his auditors were dazzled, overwhelmed by the solemnity of his words, and, as he concluded, many of them,— including some of the Trustees, presumably hardened to such displays of emotion,—had tears streaming down their cheeks. And sitting on the platform that morning was Daniel Webster!

It was appropriate that Webster should be there, for he had already become Rufus Choate's hero. When Choate had first begun to formulate his ambitions, he had decided to become a teacher. He had not been in Dartmouth very long before he wrote home, "The situation I most envy is that of a Professor in a College." As a Sophomore, he looked forward to graduate study in a foreign university, and, when the law was suggested as a possible occupation, he expressed a dislike for "the tiresome routine of a special pleader's life." That Choate was persuaded to revise this immature opinion is due mainly to his observation of Webster during the Dartmouth College Case, which was then in its final stages.

In September, 1817, when the case was being tried at Exeter, Choate was present, and, like many others, was impressed by the force and pathos of Webster's closing argument for the College. In March, 1818, it was brought before the Supreme Court of the United States, in Washington, where Webster made a shrewd appeal to John Marshall and the other Federalist judges, ending with that outburst of sentiment so dear to Dartmouth men,—"It is, Sir, a small College. And yet, there are those who love it. . . ." The Opinion delivered for the Court by Marshall in February, 1819, when Choate was a Senior, supported Webster's view, declaring that, under the Federal Constitution, no State Legislature could impair the binding force of the original Dartmouth Charter. These addresses by Webster on a subject in which the undergraduate body was so much absorbed undoubtedly influenced Choate's ideals. Although Webster, in 1819, held no public office, he was in the full glory of his physical and mental vigor, and his magnetism was almost overpowering to a susceptible youth like Choate. With a suddenness which made his family gasp, the latter announced his intention of becoming a lawyer, and from that decision, once made, he did not waver. All his life long, moreover, Choate revered Webster, defending him against criticism, helping him in financial difficulties, and standing side by side with him on great national issues. When the older statesman died, it was Rufus Choate who, in the same church where Webster had listened to him in 1819, paid him the sincerest tribute.

When a man has achieved distinction in the eyes of the world, there is often a tendency among those who knew him in his "salad days" to exaggerate the promise which he then revealed. Reminiscences "fifty years after" are usually colored by what has happened during the intervening half century. But in Choate's case it can be proved that his college mates respected him in 1819 for the keenness and grasp of his mind and,—to quote one of them,—"for the discipline and training which gave him complete command of himself and all he knew." His biographers do not need to exaggerate in order to demonstrate Choate's complete supremacy over the Dartmouth undergraduates of his generation.

Choate always loved Dartmouth. His college diploma, adorned with ribbons which are now faded, was uncovered only the other day in a box in the Choate homestead in Essex, where he had carefully put it aside for preservation. He told a friend once that he was going back to Hanover to find out whether the birds were still singing as sweetly as they had sung when he was a boy. He was Dartmouth's favorite and cherished son, and he returned more than once to speak from the platform where he had gained his earliest forensic triumph. His portrait by Ames hangs in the modern Daniel Webster Hall. A street in the village bears his name. A walk around the college will convince a visitor that, even after the lapse of more than a century, the fame of Rufus Choate is not dimmed.

For a year after his graduation, Choate, slowly recovering from his devastating illness, remained at Dartmouth as a Tutor. He had some debts which he wished to discharge before entering upon the study of the law; and there was a young lady who had aroused in him still another ambition. Beside the College Church, on the north border of the green, lived Mr. Mills Olcott, one of the local magnates, who had been Secretary and Treasurer of the Dartmouth Board of

Trustees and, in 1822, was elected a regular member of that body. He was once somewhat effusively described as "the ideal of a perfect gentleman." He had a daughter, Helen, five years younger than Rufus Choate, and said by Professor Herbert D. Foster to have been "the most charming girl in Hanover."

Although the lovely Helen was, in 1820, barely sixteen, Choate wooed and won her before another Commencement Day arrived. The undergraduates knew what was taking place, as boys usually do. The Olcott residence was a fine old house, dating back at least to 1780, and was an ornament to the Dartmouth Campus. One evening a group of roisterers, headed by Cyrus F. Smith, mounted the steeple of the College Church, only a few yards from the Olcott parlor where Choate was sitting with his sweetheart, and burst forth into an informal serenade, caroling so lustily that the whole community could hear. In the morning Tutor Choate sent for the vocal Smith and directed him to select a more decorous time and place for his musical demonstrations. Choate had not, of course, a sufficient income on which to marry, but it was well understood that he was coming back some day to carry Helen off with him. The house in which she once dwelt has recently been moved to a new site on Main Street, but it still not inappropriately bears the name of Choate.

Interested though he was in the Greek instruction which had been assigned to him, Rufus Choate was not tempted to linger at Dartmouth. Teaching seemed to him to be rather tame, and his contact with Webster had made him eager to get on with the law. Accordingly the autumn of 1820 found him at Cambridge, where he enrolled in the newly-established Harvard Law School, under a Dartmouth graduate, Chief Justice Joel Parker, one of the great jurists of his time. Harvard Law School, however, was not then taken very seriously, even by its professors. Students entered and left in a desultory manner, the average number of new men being nine each year. A few lectures were given by Asahel Stearns, the County Attorney, who held the title of University Professor of Law, and he and Parker superintended in some degree the reading of the pupils. But the Law School had inadequate quarters on the ground floor of the "Second College House" in Harvard Square, and was conducted with all the informality of an attorney's office. A Moot Court permitted students to gain practice in arguing cases, but it was held only intermittently. Indeed the school amounted to little until 1829, when it was reorganized as the Dane Law School, with a more adequate endowment.

Choate did find at Cambridge facilities for reading and study, and made the most of them. Edward Everett, then on the Harvard faculty, said of Choate, "When he was at the Law School in Cambridge, I was accustomed to meet him more frequently than any other person of his standing in the alcoves of the library of the University." Living close to Boston, he could easily go to that city to hear the trial of important cases, and he had ample opportunities for watching the leaders of the Massachusetts Bar in action. He gained in this way his first real conception of the scope and variety of the law and of the policies and methods of actual practitioners. It was a profession, as he soon discovered, which involved a knowledge, not only of legal treatises but of men.

Rufus's sister, Mary, seven years older than he, had married in 1813 Dr. Thomas Sewall, a physician of Chebacco, who had moved in 1819 to Washington, where he soon built up an excellent practice and was made Professor of Anatomy in the National Medical College. It was this friendly brother-in-law who persuaded Choate of the desirability of a year of study in the capital and secured for him a position in the office of William Wirt, President Monroe's Attorney General. Wirt, then just fifty, was one of the outstanding lawyers of the country and could have been of much assistance to Choate if he had not been seriously ill during most of the time while Choate was working under him. But

[44]

there were other successful advocates in Washington for Choate to hear. David B. Ogden, of New York, was there, and Littleton W. Tazewell, of Virginia, to say nothing of George Blake, George Sullivan, and Daniel Webster from Massachusetts, all appearing in cases in the Supreme Court, before the venerable Chief Justice Marshall. Choate was in court when William Pinkney, of Maryland, who had been for a decade the undisputed leader of the American Bar, after speaking for three consecutive days in the case of *Richard* v. *Williams,* was struck down by apoplexy and carried out unconscious, to die only a few weeks later. Speaking of Pinkney in the retrospect, Choate said, "I heard his last great argument, when, by his overwork, he snapped the cord of his life. His diction was splendidly rich, copious, and flowing. Webster followed him, but I could not help thinking he was infinitely dry, barren, and jejune." Pinkney's vehement manner, rapid speech, and powerful eloquence, combined with his logical and accurate judgment, renewed the ambition of Choate, who, in a large degree, took him as a model when he himself began to stand before judges.

The young Dartmouth graduate had enough to keep his mind from stagnation. He taught three hours every other day in a school for young ladies,—"all for cash," —and thus paid off some of his debts. In August of 1821, he wrote to his former classmate, James Marsh:

I sit three days a week in the large Congressional Library, and am studying our own extensive ante-Revolutionary history, and reading your favorite Gibbon. The only classic I can get is Ovid; and, while I am about it, let me say, too, that I read every day some chapters in an English Bible.

He was tiring of philosophy and metaphysics, in which he had formerly delighted, and was turning to more practical affairs. There were moments, of course, when he was homesick. "You can hardly imagine," he wrote to his brother, "how much I long to go back to you, and look around once more on our family circle, and on the hills, dales, and waters, of our much-loved birthplace." Again he confessed, "I like this city very little, and hope and believe I never shall make up my mind to stay here for life." New England was always before his eyes as he looked around him at the dingy barrenness of Washington. But still, by industrious reading, he tried to make himself temporarily forget Massachusetts and Helen Olcott and all that was drawing him northward.

A family tragedy settled the problem for him. Rufus's brother, Washington, four years his junior, had entered Dartmouth in 1819, where his record had been a brilliant one. The two boys, despite the difference in their ages, had been intimate companions. In February, 1822, Washington was taken ill with scarlet fever, dying within a few days. Rufus, unhappy, unable to concentrate on his books, and besought by his broken-hearted mother to come back and comfort her, at once packed up his clothes and took the long winter ride by coach back to Essex County. The next few months were indeed bitter ones, for he had no definite employment and did not know in which direction to move. The foundations of his belief had been shaken, and he was in the throes of that terrible melancholy which only the young can feel.

With gloom in his heart, he took refuge in the routine of Asa Andrews's law office in Ipswich, following this with a few months spent under the caustic Judge Cummins, in Salem. In September, 1823, he was duly admitted to practice in the Court of Common Pleas, and was entitled to seek for clients where he could find them. He was twenty-four years old; he had received a thorough scholastic training under the best of auspices; he had watched the leading men of his profession in the highest courts in the land. The time had arrived for him to demonstrate that he had not been mistaken in his choice of a career.

CHAPTER III

The Young Lawyer

*U*NLIKE Webster, Everett, Cushing, and other leading lawyers of that period, Rufus Choate was interested chiefly and primarily in his legal work. "The great purpose of Mr. Choate," said Chandler, "was to stand first in his profession; this was the main, the absorbing, aim of his life. All things else were merely auxiliary to this." From time to time he was drawn reluctantly into the service of town or state or nation; he consented to be the orator on important public occasions; he even lent the prestige of his great name to political causes,—but he always returned joyfully to the active law practice which he loved so much and in which, it may be added, he was so successful. He began modestly enough, but the field of his activities gradually widened until, as he advanced in years and experience, his reputation extended far beyond New England. Even in some of his trivial early cases in Essex County, however, he revealed the same inimitable and unique genius with which in his prime he astounded the Supreme Court of the United States.

There is a tradition that, when Choate felt himself equipped to start practice, he hung out his "shingle" in Salem, the county-seat, about twelve miles from his home in Essex, but that, after it had remained there twenty-four hours, lack of confidence induced him to take it down and transfer it to the parish of South Danvers, within the limits of the town which has been known since 1868 as Peabody. Whether the story is true or not, it is indisputable that his first office was in that hamlet. To-day Peabody is a busy and undistinguished industrial community with a population of about twenty-five thousand, most of which is foreign-born, representing many nationalities and tongues. In 1824, however, the entire South Parish included only eighteen hundred people, and there were green fields and shady walks where now are paved streets and smoky factories. "The pastures came down towards the center of the village," says an antiquarian, "and a country quiet rested over all." It was not a very prosperous place when Choate arrived, but it had for him one signal advantage,—there was no lawyer there already! Furthermore it was only two miles from Salem, so near that Choate could reach it easily by the stage, running four times a day between the two towns of Danvers and Salem, and could thus keep in touch with the county courts.

Clients came eventually, or else this biography would not have been written,—and he served them to their satisfaction. At first he was glad to accept even the most insignificant case, and devote to it the concentrated faculties of his mind. Even though the issues involved were not stupendous, he prepared his brief with meticulous care. His policy is illustrated by the notorious "dog Case," tried at Beverly, in which it was reported that "he treated the dog as though he were a lion or an elephant, and the crabbed old squire with the compliment and consideration of a chief justice." For a retaining fee of three or five dollars, he displayed before a Danvers magistrate the oratorical power which had amazed Daniel Webster at Dartmouth in 1819. It is small wonder that the people of the South Parish felt as if they were having a visitor from Olympus, for Choate was a lawyer full-grown at the very opening of his career. He showed at twenty-five the same skill which rendered him famous at forty, and the first impression which he made on judges, accustomed to the ordinary dull routine of the courtroom, was a certain guarantee of further distinction.

With the encouragement of a client or two, Choate went to Hanover in March, 1825, and there, in the Olcott House on the College Green, was married to Helen Olcott, who had waited patiently for him since his undergraduate days at Dartmouth. By temperament and disposition she was admirably suited to be his help-mate,—

> A perfect creature, nobly planned,
> To warn, to comfort, and command;
> And yet a spirit too, and bright,
> With something of an angel's light.

She survived her husband by some years, living until 1864, and after her death, a friend wrote of her that "no pressure of trial or calamity could stir the deep currents of her spirit." She was a source of soothing comfort to Rufus Choate during the troubles of his arduous professional career.

There had been hours of dejection during the preceding winter when Choate, in debt for his education and for the few volumes in his law library, had considered returning to Hog Island and tilling the soil where his ancestors had walked behind the plow. Now, however, there was a new zest to life! Clients entered his office more frequently as his reputation spread. In November, 1825, he was admitted to practice as an attorney in the Supreme Court. He could now use in the courtroom that eloquence which he had been developing in long early morning rambles through the meadows, where he addressed the unsuspecting rabbits and partridges in those tones which were later to thrill Faneuil Hall. Convinced that there would be for him no more doldrums, he bravely determined to make the world his oyster. He was no longer a novice, but a master.

The persons who consulted Rufus Choate soon learned that he took all his cases very seriously. He was like a physician who gives to an attack of chicken pox the same scrupulous attention that he bestows upon a patient with advanced tuberculosis. Stories of all sorts illustrating this conscientiousness have been handed down from generation to generation in Essex County until there has been evolved a kind of Choate legend. Once he was called out at night to draft a will for an aged client who lived several miles away. When the complicated business was arranged and he was home in bed, he lay awake, as was his custom then and later, running over in his restless mind what he had done during the day. . . . Suddenly he remembered that he had inadvertently omitted a phrase which should have been inserted in order to make the document complete. Knowing that the testator was dying, Choate jumped up, dressed, and, in the midst of a heavy storm, rode back to his client, explained the situation, and drew the proper codicil.

I find, fully reported in the Salem *Gazette*, the trial, in 1825, at Ipswich, of one Ammi Smith, who, it was alleged, had obstructed the highway with three cords of wood, so that John C. Cooper, driving a load of cider barrels to Salem, hit the pile, with the result that an empty barrel fell on his mare and lamed her. Here was a case for Rufus Choate's genius! As attorney for Smith, he obtained a verdict for the defendant, with costs at $3.98. One can imagine the size of the fee which the defendant's lawyer charged!

Rufus Choate began his career in an era when there was no prejudice against lawyers who accepted retainers from persons accused of crime. In the twentieth century, few attorneys care to interest themselves in criminal practice, and the ablest men undoubtedly prefer to specialize in what is known as corporation work. Such lawyers as Webster and Lincoln, however, were frequently engaged in criminal suits. Choate, in his younger days, enjoyed that kind of practice, and came to be recognized in Essex County as "the great criminal lawyer," until he had almost a monopoly in that field. It was not until he reached middle life that he turned by preference to the civil law.

We are fortunate in having an excellent description of the first time he appeared in Salem,—in the Mumford Case, tried before Police Magistrate Ezekiel Savage. Choate, whose reputation was already spreading beyond South Danvers, was employed to defend some young men of respectable families in his own community who were charged with having incited a riot in a negro dance-hall on the Boston turnpike. The courtroom on the second floor of a building in the center of the town was packed with a diversified audience of sailors, clerks, supercargoes, and others who had little to do; but, as reports of the trial were spread outside, even substantial citizens fought their way into the crowded room to hear the eloquent attorney from South Danvers. Choate conducted his defense with cleverness, examining witnesses as if he had had years of experience; and, when the moment arrived for his argument, he seemed to dignify the case and its sordid surroundings until it assumed the aspect of something far greater than it had appeared to be before. Just as Mrs. Wharton has made the bruised Ethan Frome a supremely tragic figure, so Choate transformed the commonplace into something heroic. His ordinarily stolid listeners sat as if magnetized, unaware that they were hearing a voice which was to bring fame to Essex County. The newspapers praised the speech as "an extraordinary and wholly matchless performance," which "lifted up" those who were in the audience. It is this phrase *lifted up* which one finds so often used to describe what Choate accomplished then and later in seizing upon an apparently petty matter and making it stand out as of cosmic significance. His clients were triumphantly acquitted, and his fame was made at the Essex County Bar. Henceforth no one in that vicinity was unaware of Rufus Choate.

Choate's first appearance before the Supreme Judicial Court was in the case of *Jones* v. *Andover*, in November, 1827, before Chief Justice Isaac Parker. The plaintiff, whose attorneys were Saltonstall and Merrill, had brought an action to recover damages for injury due to a highway in Andover which was out of repair. The question at issue was dependent on a technicality,—whether the term "highway" employed as a statute of 1786 included "town-ways." Choate, arguing for the town of Andover, did his best to prove that a "town-way" was not, strictly speaking, a "highway." He was not able to convince the court, and he lost the case, but his presentation of his cause did him credit. In 1829, acting for the town of Andover again, Choate petitioned for a new trial, but the request was denied.

If this had been a trial before a jury, Choate would probably have won his case, for, even in those apprentice days, it was with a jury that he achieved his most notable triumphs. He had already developed a peculiar and highly individual style of speaking which was soon to be associated with his personality and which we must later analyze in detail. He had learned both how to convince and how to persuade, how to seize upon what was important and to neglect what was unessential, how to marshal his evidence as a general directs his troops, concentrating them upon the enemy's weakest defenses. Even while the jurymen were resolving to resist his plausible eloquence, they were yielding to the witchery of his appeal. It was said that, while he remained in Essex County, no jury ever brought in a verdict of "Guilty" against a client defended by him. This is doubtless an exaggeration, but it illustrates the reputation which he had acquired in only a few years.

Even the surest case seemed to go to pieces on the rocks of Choate's oratory. A South Danvers man named Jefferds had been indicted for stealing a flock of turkeys. The proof of guilt seemed to be overwhelming, and the county attorney, who had prepared himself with great care against his redoubtable opponent, was sure of victory; yet there was one dissenting juror, who had been struck by Choate's argument for the defense. It became a local *cause celebre*, and, at each successive court, inquisitive people would ask, "When are the turkeys coming up again?" The fourth trial was held at Ipswich, only a short distance from Choate's old home at Essex, and his friends drove over to hear him. It was the kind of scene which Choate loved,—the courthouse jammed with visitors and the

[56]

atmosphere tense with excitement. He himself was at his best, with everything in his favor except the evidence. Witness after witness testified against his client; and yet, when Choate had finished speaking, there was one juror still who held out, and a verdict could not be secured. It was as if Choate had exercised a power of hypnotism over the man's will. It is no wonder that the prosecuting attorney, in despair, entered a *nolle prosequi* and let the offender go free.

Sometimes a whimsical turn of phrase would attract the attention of the jurymen and gain their sympathies. A mischievous youngster who had annoyed a man named Adams by stealing apples, pushing over stone fences, and letting down pasture bars, was one day caught in the act by the irate farmer and swung around by the hair of his head. The father of the scapegrace prosecuted Adams, and Choate appeared for the defendant. He appealed to the jury by describing the act of chastisement as merely "a little paternal stretching of the neck, which perchance may save this froward lad from a final and more eventful stretching." The delightful implication of the words made the jurors smile, and Choate had won his case.

It must not be imagined, however, that Choate was a mere trickster, who relied upon the quickness of his wits. He never accepted a case without bestowing upon it the most exhaustive study, giving to it the same patient research which he had shown in his work at Dartmouth. Adversaries who had not fortified themselves with facts were certain to be overwhelmed. Once started in a cause, he was a ganglion of nervous energy, never relaxing, never allowing his thoughts to wander, until the crisis was over. He would often sit up all night before the trial, mastering every phase of the subject upon which he was for the moment concentrating; and in the courtroom the next day he would become so wrought up in his address to the jury that the perspiration would stand out in great drops on his forehead, and, when he sat down, he would have to wrap himself up all over to avoid taking cold. The tremendous expenditure of vitality left him usually with a sick headache, but he was quick to recuperate when the strain was over. Even in those younger days he was described as "liberal of work, impatient of repose, intense in action, sparing of recreation." When a man of quick intuitions and keen intelligence is also industrious, he is not likely to fail in his profession. Choate had native talent, no doubt, but it was supplemented by a prodigious amount of what would have seemed to the average observer mere drudgery. No lawyer in this country ever devoted himself more whole-heartedly to his vocation.

In 1828 Choate had found South Danvers too small

a field for his expanding powers. Clients were hunting him out from all over Essex County,—from Newburyport and Andover and Ipswich,—and he saw the advisability of locating at the center of affairs. Accordingly, he moved, with his wife and his little two-year-old daughter, Catherine Bell, to Salem, then a busy maritime community of approximately fourteen thousand people. Although its golden days were passing and it was being overshadowed by Boston, Salem ships still flew the American flag in every port of the world. The Custom House at Derby Wharf, built in 1819, was a hive of industry,—not the melancholy refuge for derelicts which Hawthorne described some years later,—and in 1832 the Salem vessels in the deep-water trade numbered 111. Society in Salem, although Rufus Choate saw little of it, was gay and witty, and there was plenty of money to spend in luxurious living. But for Choate it was primarily the place where the Supreme Judicial Court held its county sessions and where clients might be expected to flock to his door.

He came to Salem, poor in purse but with a reputation which already extended through Essex County,—a young man of whom wagging tongues prophesied great things. He was even then a striking figure, nearly six feet in height, of brown complexion, with dark and gloomy eyes and a profusion of curly hair which he was at no pains to brush. He had then what he was seldom later to enjoy,—robust physical health. He was careless in his dress, but not slovenly. His clothes, although the coat might be fastened negligently by a single button, were invariably of the best material, and his linen was always neat. One who remembered him at this period described his "very democratic attire, with cheap pantaloons, a long slouchy vest, a blue coat with metallic buttons (and quite too small for him), and a black cravat, much resembling a string, thrown around rather than tied on his neck." Whipple called him "an Apollo with a slouch." Salem was used to the magnificent bearing and regal demeanor of Daniel Webster, with his forehead like that of Olympian Jove's, "to threaten and command"; but Choate was so weirdly unique that he stimulated even the most jaded imagination. He was like nobody else that the town had known. He would say the most preposterous things in such a half-grave manner that his hearers would be convulsed with merriment while he himself appeared lugubriously solemn. Although he never laughed boisterously, he had a droll humor and a keen sense of the ridiculous. Choate, it was perceived, was different from others not merely in degree, but also in kind. A judge who was acquainted with both Webster and Choate expressed the contrast perfectly. "Webster seemed to be a good deal like other folks, only there was more of him. But Choate was peculiar,—a strange, beautiful product of our time, not to be measured by reference to ordinary men." Choate had what is called, rather vaguely, personality, an inexplicable and altogether indefinable factor, but one vitally essential to success.

It did not take long for Rufus Choate to establish himself in Salem. He soon became known in the Salem bookstores, especially in that of John M. Ives, where he could usually be found late on any afternoon, after the courts and offices were closed, prowling eagerly around the shelves. He was thrown at once into open competition with opponents not to be despised. There were young men like himself,—Caleb Cushing, the precocious and ambitious Admirable Crichton from Newburyport, and Robert Rantoul, Jr., the Beverly aristocrat who dared to enter political life as a Democrat and an adherent of Andrew Jackson. There were the old campaigners: John Pickering, of Beverly, and Leverett Saltonstall, of Salem, under both of whom Rantoul had studied; Ebenezer Moseley, of Newburyport, in whose office Cushing received his practical training; and John Varnum, of Haverhill, then the Congressman from Essex North District. Against these men, and others like Shillaber, Lunt, Lord, Ward, and Merrill, Choate battled in friendly rivalry. There was every incentive for a lawyer to do his best, and he gave himself up to the struggle which meant the survival of the fittest. Within a year or two he was being retained in more cases in the Court of Common Pleas than any other attorney in Essex County, and every defendant in a criminal action tried to engage his services. He appeared regularly also at the sessions of the Supreme Judicial Court, often associated with other lawyers. Although rarely unsuccessful in a jury trial, Choate frequently lost before the Supreme Court Judges, who were less susceptible to his persuasive manner,—especially Chief Justice Isaac Parker, who usually presided.

Even if this book were being written for lawyers only, it would be impossible to deal with the numerous cases in the *Reports of the Supreme Judicial Court* in which Choate was employed as counsel during the years from 1828 to 1834, while he was a resident of Salem. They represent every phase of legal practice, and he had a chance to gain the widest possible experience. He won his first victory in the Supreme Judicial Court in April, 1828, in the case of *Cogswell* v. *The Essex Mill Corporation*, representing the defendants against Saltonstall and Shillaber, attorneys for the plaintiffs. It was naturally encouraging for him to see that he could hold his own against such seasoned veterans, but there had never been any doubt that he would forge to the front of the Essex County Bar. And whether he won or lost, his client knew that Choate had done his best.

It was during his residence in Salem that Choate was employed as an advisory but silent counsel to assist Daniel Webster in the trials of Joseph Knapp, Jr., and Francis Knapp for the murder of Captain Joseph White,—one of the notorious crimes of the century. Rantoul, with characteristic courage, was willing to act as counsel for the defense. At the first trial of Francis Knapp, as principal, the jury disagreed; but, when a second attempt was ordered, Webster delivered the famous speech in which occurs the most dramatic description of a murder ever presented in a courtroom. The jury, unable to resist the appeal of Webster, brought in a verdict of "Guilty," and Joseph was convicted some weeks later. Choate had sat by Webster's side throughout the proceedings and had offered some valuable suggestions. If only he had been employed for the defense against the mighty Webster, Essex County would have been treated to the most spectacular legal contest ever held within its borders, and possibly Choate might have achieved the impossible and saved the Knapps from the gallows.

While he was thus becoming known to a wider and wider circle in Essex County, his family life was going on quietly, with domestic joys and tragedies. On

[63]

October 25, 1828, just after he had moved to Salem, an infant son died at birth, and in May, 1830, his daughter, Catherine Bell, died just before her fourth birthday. Another daughter, Helen Olcott, had been born just a few weeks earlier, and was destined to live to a fine old age. She later married Joseph Mills Bell, Esquire, and was the last of the family to survive. A second daughter, born on December 15, 1831, also grew up to be the comfort of her parents, living with them to the close of their days. The only son, Rufus, was born on May 14, 1834, but he died in young manhood and never married. Two other daughters were born to Rufus Choate after he had moved to Boston: Miriam Foster, born October 2, 1835, and Caroline, born September 15, 1837, who died in early childhood. The percentage of children to live was not large. Three of the seven died in infancy or childhood. Only two were married, and of these only one had children; and the only male heir had no children to carry on the name.

CHAPTER IV

The Lawyer in Politics

*I*T was very difficult for a really successful lawyer
in the first half of the nineteenth century to keep out
of politics, and most of the leading statesmen of that
period had been originally members of the bar. A careful checking of members of the Massachusetts General
Court and of representatives in Congress between 1789
and 1850 would show that a majority of them had legal
training. Webster, Levi Lincoln, John Davis, Cushing,
and Rantoul,—to mention only the more important
names,—were drawn sooner or later away from their
law offices and into political careers. So it was also with
Rufus Choate. The difference was that Choate never
solicited any legislative position. When he was elected,
he felt it his duty to serve; but the office always had to
seek the man. It may be said truthfully that he was
seldom really happy away from his desk and his clients.
The more he saw of legislative machinery, the less he
cared to be connected with it. And yet, in spite of this
distaste for politics, Choate moved from one office to

another, serving successively as Representative in the Massachusetts General Court, State Senator, Congressman, and Senator of the United States.

One of his most dangerous competitors at the Bar of Essex County was Caleb Cushing, who was three months younger than Choate, but, being remarkably precocious, had graduated from Harvard two years before his rival had taken his degree at Dartmouth. Cushing had been admitted to practice and had already made a good start in his profession before Choate settled in South Danvers. Meeting in the courts, the two young men had become friends and had, in fact, outlined a project for a comprehensive digest of the *English Year Books*, each preparing a rough sketch of the portions which he would undertake. Unfortunately they were soon so busy that neither could carry out his share of the plan. Thus the legal fraternity was deprived of a reference work which would have displayed on its title page the names of two of America's greatest advocates.

In 1825, Cushing was a member of the Massachusetts General Court from Newburyport, and gained so much distinction that Choate was moved to emulate him. When, therefore, the latter was nominated in the spring of 1826 as Representative from South Danvers, he accepted and was readily elected. He had already served on the local School Committee, and

[66]

everybody knew "lawyer Choate." It cannot be said
that Choate drew much attention to himself on Beacon
Hill. We know, from his own statement, that his first
speech on the floor was in favor of a bill requiring a
higher standard of education for teachers in the common schools. He was a member of a Special Committee
to report "on the depressed condition of our woolen
manufactures,"—a fact which indicates that New England a century ago was having its industrial problems.
But he did not attend the legislative sessions with regu-
larity, for he was too much occupied in getting established in the law. After all, he had to earn his living.
Cushing, who had been promoted to the Senate, commented in his *Journal* on Choate's practice of attending
but intermittently to his legislative duties,—"neglecting
the ordinary business of the House, & only making an
elaborate speech now and then." Cushing, who never
neglected anything, concluded sagely that Choate could
thus acquire the reputation of being a man of talent, but
could not have any stable influence as a member of the
House. This was undeniably true. But it is equally
certain that Choate, deep down in his heart, scorned
being "a business member of the House." There were
other aims in that fertile brain of his, and he was well
aware of what he was doing.

In spite of Choate's irregularity of attendance, he

[67]

was reëlected in 1827 and appeared at the two sessions in June, 1827, and January, 1828. He was a member of a Committee appointed to consider how Electors for President and Vice President should be chosen, and he was Chairman of a Select Committee on the Pauper Laws. These were not positions of importance, but they were all that his rather lukewarm interest in state politics deserved. He was a candidate for State Senator in April, 1828, and received some complimentary votes from his South Danvers friends, but the other sections of Essex County ignored him and he lost by a wide margin. A year later, after he had moved to Salem, he again ran for State Senator and was easily elected. When the Senate was organized in May, 1829, Choate was named as a member of the important Committee on the Judiciary and of the Committee on Bills in the Second Reading. Evidently he was slowly becoming better known to the political leaders.

When his term as Senator expired in the spring of 1830, Choate was so much absorbed in the extension of his practice in Salem that he refused to allow himself to be renominated. But he could not, with his ability, evade the public eye, for he was a familiar figure on Essex Street. His fame as an orator had been early established in South Danvers, where he had twice delivered addresses on Independence Day, one of them being before the Danvers Light Infantry, in which, like a good citizen, he had enlisted. On July 4, 1828, in Salem, Choate spoke in the North Church, his oration, according to the Salem *Gazette*, being "original, bold, and eloquent." He had become a member of the Salem School Committee and a Manager of the Salem Lyceum. Indeed, he had reached a point where he was being "mentioned" for nearly every local honor.

Just then an opportunity presented itself which a rising young lawyer could not afford to ignore, especially as it was not likely soon to occur again. The Congressman from Essex South District was then Benjamin Williams Crowninshield, who had been Secretary of the Navy from 1814 to 1818, under Presidents Madison and Monroe, and was just completing his fourth consecutive term. Connected with one of the old and wealthy shipping families of Salem, he was a person of influence in commercial circles; but he was nearly sixty, and there were those who felt that some one more aggressive ought to represent Essex South during the struggle of New England to hold back the rising tide of Jacksonism. The fact that Crowninshield had been a silent member of Congress was not in his favor. Who was better equipped to be his successor than young lawyer Choate, who was certainly not silent,—who had served an apprenticeship in the General Court, who had

[69]

shown himself to be an inspiring speaker, and who was known to have the approval of the great Senator Webster himself?

In October, therefore, the National Republicans, in their District Convention at the Lafayette Coffee House in Salem, nominated Choate for Congress. He had done nothing whatever to promote his own candidacy,—that had been in the hands of his old South Danvers friends,—but he had agreed not to decline. Opportunity was speaking:

> Those who doubt or hesitate
> Condemned to failure, penury, and woe,
> Seek me in vain and uselessly implore,
> I answer not, and I return no more.

If he had refused, some one else would have been singled out to oppose Crowninshield, and thus his chance of getting to Congress would, as he wrote his friend Marsh, have been postponed for at least ten years. When he was formally accepted, he learned that Crowninshield, annoyed by the presumption of the native of Hog Island, had resolved to run on an independent ticket. Choate was precipitated unexpectedly into the midst of a contested election.

In the course of the noisy and somewhat vituperative struggle which followed, Choate, who was a man of

Rufus Choate, from a Contemporary Engraving

peace, was taught, for the first time in his career, what abuse was like. He was accused of a "vaulting ambition." It was intimated that he intended to use the House of Representatives merely to further his own selfish ends and that he was a resident of Salem only as a transient, stopping there merely while he "oated his horse" on the way to Boston. He was praised by his supporters as being "a decided friend of Henry Clay and of the American System; and, at the same time, strongly devoted to the Commercial and Navigating Interests of this country." Both Choate and Crowninshield held virtually the same political views, like loyal anti-Jackson men. The contest was not one of principles. It was a clash between the old and rather worn-out aristocracy and the newer generation, and the result could not be in doubt. . . . . Furthermore Choate himself was not a person whom anybody could dislike. He was so modest, so attractive, so entirely frank and generous, that he gained votes while he was being denounced. At the close of the short and intense campaign, Choate was the winner by a majority of more than five hundred. Replying to the congratulations of his friend, Marsh, Choate said, "I hardly dare yet look the matter in the face. Political life,—between us,— is no part of my plan, although I trust I shall aim in good faith to perform the duties *temporarily* and *incidentally* thus assigned." It was a mild kind of enthusiasm for a newly-elected Congressman to display.

Rufus Choate was not, however, a man who neglected responsibilities, and he started with his habitual diligence to prepare himself, laying out a thorough course of study on all the vital issues of the hour. In that baffling hieroglyphic handwriting which was the despair of his correspondents, he outlined the subjects which he must master, including the public lands, the tariff, the Indians, and,—most significant of all,—"the cause of the excitement in the Southern States." He analyzed President Jackson's Message paragraph by paragraph, as he would have made a brief for a law case. He made a thorough examination into the history, commercial situation, and immediate needs of his districts. Already a good public speaker, he endeavored to perfect himself by perusing the masterpieces of classical and modern eloquence, training his voice for the tumults of Congressional debates, and making his manner as pleasing as possible. He set for himself a program of daily physical exercise for the maintenance of his good health. It is worth noting that he and his friend, Caleb Cushing, pursued almost precisely the same routine of careful preparation for their Washington careers. These two brilliant Essex County youths

supplemented their quickness of intellect by long hours
of reading at their desks:

> They, while their companions slept,
> Were toiling upward through the night.

Choate took a room in the national capital on the
third floor of the house of his brother-in-law, Dr.
Sewall, from two windows of which he could look out
"upon the shores of Virginia, the setting sun, and the
grave of Washington," and where he could pursue his
studies "at a long table,—perhaps the most desirable of
luxuries." A lady asked him why he did not bring Mrs.
Choate to Washington. "I assure you, madam," he
replied, "that I have spared no pains to induce her to
come. I have even offered to pay half her expenses."
Hotel facilities in the capital were not precisely what
they are to-day, and Choate was undoubtedly wise in
leaving his family in their comfortable Salem home.

As a Congressman, Rufus Choate did not take an
active share in the daily routine of legislation. Continuing the policy which he had adopted in the Massachusetts General Court, he spoke at least once on every
important question before the House, and he was absolutely fearless in expressing his views; but he avoided
as far as possible the dull labor of the committee room,

and he shunned clerical work. He had no taste whatever for what Edward Everett called "electioneering legerdemain,"—that is, he simply could not bring himself to carry on with his constituents all the burdensome correspondence in which some of his colleagues rather reveled. He was disdainful of the delicate arts by which advancement was sought and often obtained. Indeed it was quite evident to those in his confidence that he regarded his office as an unavoidable and not altogether agreeable interruption to his professional and literary career. Even while he walked to the Capitol, he carried his Shakspere in his pocket, and he construed a few lines of Greek and Latin each morning.

Latin and Greek, however, are not absolutely essential to advancement in American politics, and there was the business of the session to be transacted. After the long journey of nearly a week from Salem, he took his seat on Monday, December 5, 1831, as a member of a Massachusetts delegation which included the old statesman, John Quincy Adams, the scholarly Edward Everett,—just beginning his fourth term,—George N. Briggs,—later the "Guvener B" of Lowell's *Biglow Papers*,—and John Davis. In the House there were few other men whose names are well known to-day, although one future President, James Knox Polk, was among them, as well as the poetic Richard Henry

[74]

Wilde, the witty Tom Corwin, of Ohio, and the fiery
George McDuffie, of South Carolina. When the Standing Committees were announced, Choate was without an
assignment, but he was later given a place on the Special
Committee on Patents,—an appointment which no one
of his colleagues was likely to envy. For some weeks he
sat silent, watching the course of events, listening while
men less gifted than he discussed such varied subjects as
the Chicksaw Treaty, the disposal of Washington's remains, the Bank of the United States, and Amy Dardin's
horse, and voting regularly with Adams and Everett
against the Jacksonian Democrats on every roll call. At
last, on April 7, 1832, Choate gained the floor while the
topic of Revolutionary Pensions were being debated and
made a stirring plea, very creditable to the son of a
Revolutionary veteran, for a bill providing for an extension of pensions. It was a good speech, if not a great
one, and there were passages in which he indulged his
fondness for rhetoric:

May you not, ought you not, to multiply and present to
those who shall serve you in these great crises, inducement to
serve you well? You give them wages, bounties, promotion,
swords, and medals. May you not, and ought you not, to be
able to point them also to the laurels which a grateful country
has wreathed around other brows, and to the glory which
covers the living and the dead of other fields? May you not

secure future service by generously rewarding past service? May you not honor the dead, and pension the aged, that the living and the young may be stimulated to an equally salutary emulation?

The chief issue of the Twenty-Second Congress, however, was the tariff, a matter of supreme importance to the new manufacturing industries of New England. The old mercantile families in the Essex County seaports were investing their money in textile mills, and some of those men who had opposed a protective tariff in 1816 had become staunch advocates of Henry Clay's "American System." Even Daniel Webster, the high priest of the National Republicans in Massachusetts, had voted for the "Tariff of Abominations" in 1828. This measure had been obnoxious to the Southern states; furthermore the fact that the National Debt was about to be extinguished made it advisable to reduce the revenue so that the Treasury would not pile up a surplus. As soon as the session opened, therefore, a vigorous discussion commenced. Choate wrote home that the Southerners hated New England, thinking "that the tariff raises the prices of their purchases, for the sole benefit of the New England manufacturer." By this date, Choate, influenced by Webster and by the fact that his own district was profiting by the policy, had come to believe that "infant industries" must be coddled. If he had not spoken on the tariff and fought for the "American System," a large part of his constituency would never have forgiven him.

After a prolonged debate, a tariff act, sponsored by John Quincy Adams, Chairman of the Committee on Manufactures, was introduced. Adams had the broadmindedness to admit that the Tariff of 1828 was unjust to the South and that a reduction in rates was due the planters of that section. His own plan was a reasonably equitable one, but it was not fully endorsed by any of the cliques which it would affect. As for Choate, he opposed it unreservedly, as did most of his colleagues from Massachusetts; and on June 13, a day of heat like that of a fiery furnace, he rose in the afternoon to present his protest. When he began, there were few in the Hall of Representatives, most of the hot and tired members having gone out for cooler air and refreshment. As he got under way, others drifted in, until the seats were full. Then Nature herself conspired to provide him with a sensational background. A thunder-storm, rolling up the Potomac, burst over the dome of the Capitol. Choate, who had a nervous dread of electrical disturbances, stood directly under the central skylight, his face pale as ashes and his body tense and quivering under the strain. Every eye was fastened upon him as he went on, amid the deepening gloom, his sonorous periods punctuated by rumbles in the clouds, while the occasional flashes illumined his spectral countenance so that he resembled some warlock weaving a spell. Then, as quickly as it had arrived, the storm moved on, the grayness cleared away, the thunder receded, and Choate's manner, in harmony with the change in nature, became quieter, until he closed in softly modulated tones, like the still small voice after a hurricane. Those who were present never forgot that moment. When the speech was over, they crowded around to offer congratulations, and then the orator hurried home to bathe his forehead with camphor and lie down with the splitting headache which always followed one of his unusual efforts.

Aside from the splendor of its delivery, Choate's argument was not remarkable, and the sectional character of its appeal was not calculated to make it popular outside of New England. He devoted himself principally to the manufacturers of his state, who, as he said, were "now menaced by an abandonment of that policy which had made them what they are and placed them where they are." Replying to the threat of secession, he said courageously and frankly:

South Carolina has no more right, and no fairer pretext, to leave the Union if you continue this policy than Massachusetts has to go if you abandon it. . . . South Carolina stood out against the law. She asks you to repeal it to-day because it does her a great injury. Massachusetts asks you not to repeal it to-day, because that will do her a great injury. Where is the difference? . . . Sir, there is no more principle on the South Carolina side of this controversy than there is on the Massachusetts side of it. She would repeal the law, to benefit her cotton planters. We would retain it, to benefit our cotton, woolen, and glass manufacturers, and keep up the wages of free labor.

Whatever our views on the general question, we must agree that Choate's statement was an honest one. In spite of his protests, however, the measure was passed in late June, with Choate, Everett, Davis, and Briggs all opposing it, averse to compromise. When Congress adjourned on July 16, the member from Essex South returned gladly to his family and the cooling east winds which mitigate the summer heat of the North Shore. His record had not been brilliant. Two speeches during a long session do not constitute any exceptional achievement. But he had satisfied the voters of his district, for his predecessor had made no speeches at all.

During the autumn, while the Presidential campaign was being carried on, Choate was hopeful that Jackson might be defeated. In Massachusetts, indeed, Clay had 33,000 to Jackson's 14,500,—but politicians had long been aware that Massachusetts was far from representing the sentiment of the nation on any subject. The vote in the Electoral College was 219 for Jackson against 49 for Clay. Choate wrote Everett after the result had been announced: "The news from the voting states blows over us like a great cold storm. I suppose all is lost, and that the map may be rolled up for twelve years to come. Happy if when it is opened again, no state shall be missing." Choate himself had been returned to Congress without opposition,—Crowninshield having meanwhile moved to Boston,—and was apparently compelled to continue in his political career, whether he wished to do so or not.

The second session of the Twenty-Second Congress, opening on December 3, 1832, was due to close on the following March 3, and ordinarily there would have been little real business accomplished. But defiant South Carolina had passed in November a Nullification Ordinance declaring the Tariff Bill of 1832 to be null and void, and the issue of the integrity of the Union was immediately raised. In January, 1833, President Jackson, who had already written a proclamation notifying the citizens of South Carolina that "disunion by armed force is *treason*," asked Congress to pass an act giving him sufficient powers to meet the crisis. Meanwhile the so-called "Compromise Tariff" measure of 1833 was introduced and discussed for days and weeks. Choate's speech on the subject, made on January 15, took a stand against any attempt to frame an entirely new tariff bill at that session. He objected to the Compromise Tariff on the ground that it virtually overturned the American protective system, and that Congress was taking this step only through fear of what might happen in South Carolina. Despite his protest, however, the Compromise Tariff Bill was passed, with most of the Massachusetts delegation voting against it. Two or three days later the "Revenue Collection Bill,"—better known as the Force Bill,—authorizing Jackson to take any necessary steps to save the Union, was put through by a large vote, Choate voting with his Massachusetts colleagues in its favor. The emergency had been met, but not without concession on the part of the Federal Government,—concessions which Rufus Choate would have been glad to withhold. Writing on January 29, he said, "One single mistake now, any yielding, anything short of a dead march up to the whole outermost limit of Constitutional power, and the Federal Government is contemptible forever." These words must be remembered when, later on, we have to face squarely the charge of cowardice sometimes brought against Rufus Choate.

The one really exciting question during the first session of the Twenty-Third Congress concerned the

Bank of the United States. During the late summer of
1833, the new Secretary of the Treasury, at the request
of President Jackson, had issued a recess order stopping
all government deposits with the Bank or any of its
branches. The Whig Senate, enraged, passed a vote of
censure upon the President; but the House was now
Jacksonian by a large majority, and there was no redress
there for those who were favorably disposed to the
Bank. Choate, continuing his policy of speaking at
least once on each important topic before the House,
secured the floor on March 28, 1834, for a long discussion of the subject, presenting a closely reasoned argument for restoring the custody of public moneys to the
Bank of the United States. He had taken pains to
investigate the problem in all its complex details, and,
although everybody, including himself, realized that his
speech was futile, he was listened to with attention.
Some idea of the impression which he produced may be
obtained from the confession of Ben Hardin, of Kentucky, a rough and ready duelist, who was as little
likely as any man to be moved by sentiment. It was
Hardin's established custom never to lend an ear to arguments upon the same side of the question that he later
intended to uphold; but, when, having discovered upon
what topic Choate proposed to speak, he had taken his
hat in his hand and was about to retire to a committee

room, his attention was arrested by the sentence which the member from Massachusetts was finishing. "That moment," he went on, "was fatal to my resolution. I became charmed by the music of his voice, and was captivated by the power of his eloquence, and found myself wholly unable to move until the last word of his beautiful speech had been delivered." John Quincy Adams, who was not given to effusiveness, wrote in his *Diary* that evening that it was "the most eloquent speech of the session, and, in the course of reasoning, altogether impressive and original." It was indeed a good speech and reads well to-day in the small type and uninspiring pages of Gales and Seaton's *Reports*. But it accomplished nothing. Once again Choate had been eloquent in support of "lost causes." It may have been this incident which clinched his decision to leave political life and devote all his time to the law. As soon as the session closed in June, 1834, he resigned his seat. The vacancy was quickly filled by the election of Stephen C. Phillips, of Salem, one of Choate's friends, who had served acceptably in the Massachusetts General Court.

Of Choate's disgust with politics at that particular moment there can be no doubt. As a member of the minority party in the House, he could have little share in legislation, and he could not stir his Congressional colleagues as he could move a jury. Democratic representatives from Virginia would listen to his speeches and applaud courteously, but they continued to vote for the policies of Andrew Jackson. Furthermore Choate had not been really happy in Washington. He had won the respect of everybody whom he met, but he could not endure the mesh of intrigue in which he found himself entangled. Whipple said, "Everything mean and base in politics Choate absolutely loathed. To him 'machine politics' were equally a bore and a blunder." No man was ever less versed in the devious arts of the politician. But the chief motive for his resignation was probably his determination to seek in Boston a wider field for his professional talents. Urged by Webster and Everett, and not uninfluenced by financial considerations, he proposed to try his fortune in the metropolis of New England. He was, of course, leaving an established position for a venture which had its hazards, but he knew most of the lawyers with whom he would have to compete, and he was not afraid.

Choate had not allowed his Congressional career to take him entirely away from the law. In November, 1830, just after his election as Representative, he was retained to defend Philip Finnegan, charged with obtaining fraudulently from Jonathan Nichols, of Danvers, four bushels of ashes to the value of one dollar and twelve pounds of grease valued at fifty cents.

In what the Salem *Register* called an "able and spirited defense," Choate admitted that his client had committed "a piece of unjustifiable trickery,—a shabby and ungentlemanly affair, to be sure, but not the crime with which he is charged"; and the jury brought in a verdict of "Not Guilty!" A few days later he appeared for the defendant in the trial of Benjamin B. Balch for stealing one side of harness leather. The prisoner was convicted, but had in the interval absconded, and was not to be found when sentence was to be imposed.

Cases like these do seem ridiculous, in the light of Choate's later fame, but it must be remembered that he was still a young practitioner eager for experience. And they were not the only suits in which he was concerned. During the years while he was spending the winters in Washington, he was pleading regularly before the Massachusetts Supreme Judicial Court, often in cases which, even to laymen, have a great deal of interest. At the November term, in 1832, Choate appeared for the plaintiff in *Wonson* v. *Sayward*, a slander suit brought because Sayward had accused Wonson of robbing a dead body cast ashore from a wreck. Choate was successful in this instance in getting Chief Justice Shaw to order a new trial. He represented the defendants in the celebrated case of *Murdock* v. *Trustees of Phillips Academy*, in which Professor James Murdock,

[85]

who had been removed by the Trustees as Brown Professor of Sacred Rhetoric in Andover Theological Seminary, sued to recover a portion of his salary, on the ground that his removal was not legal until it had been confirmed by the Board of Visitors of that institution. In this case, as in others, Choate was on the losing side, but it was felt that he had done his best under the circumstances; and clients continued to come.

It was not solely as an advocate that Choate's reputation was growing. He had also acquired prestige as a platform orator. In 1833, he prepared with great care a lecture with a formidable title,—*The Importance of Illustrating New England History by a Series of Romances Like the Waverley Novels*,—which he delivered, not only in Salem, but also in other towns in Essex County. The Age of Lyceums was just beginning, and Rufus Choate, while never having the leisure for any large number of engagements, was one of the first in that field in which such men as Everett and Wendell Phillips were later to be so popular. I venture to say that even that elusive person, the "average reader," will be entertained to-day by Choate's lecture, both for its generous appreciation of Walter Scott and for its sympathetic picture of the New England Puritans and the lives which they led. This latter topic he developed still more elaborately in an address on *The Colonial Age of*

New England, prepared for the two hundredth anniversary of the settlement of the town of Ipswich, held on August 16, 1834.

If Rufus Choate knew Nathaniel Hawthorne in Salem, neither has recorded the acquaintance. Hawthorne, shy and morbid, had returned from Bowdoin College in 1825 to the old Manning House on Herbert Street, where he lived like a recluse, in a room under the eaves with only a single window, going out to walk only at night. He himself said that hardly twenty people in the town were aware of his existence, for poverty, diffidence, and pride kept him withdrawn from society. And yet there was in Choate something which would have understood Hawthorne if the two could have been brought together.

During the summer of 1834 Rufus Choate, who was a Mason and deplored the Antimasonic agitation which was then apparently so dangerous in American politics, rode with Caleb Cushing through Eastern Massachusetts, trying to persuade Masonic lodges to make concessions in view of a violent antagonism to them which had suddenly sprung up. Choate and Cushing had some success in their mission, but within a few months the excitement had died down, and the newly-formed Whig Party, that inchoate organization of anti-Jackson men, had come into being. Of that

[87]

party Choate was one of the earliest members, and he stood by it until it had almost died of inanition. A strange party! Formed of various elements which had amalgamated chiefly through their hatred of Andrew Jackson, it was headed by men of ability, like Clay, Webster, Everett, Adams, and Choate, but it lacked consistency and direction.

In the autumn of 1834, then, Rufus Choate moved, with his family of a wife, two daughters, and an infant son, to Boston, then a city of about seventy thousand people, second only to New York as a seat of commerce. He was already familiar with Boston, and there were friends to welcome him there: Daniel Webster, his model as a statesman, and Jeremiah Mason, and Edward Everett, soon to be Governor of the Commonwealth. All the omens seemed favorable. The story of his life thus far had been one of widening circles. From Hog Island, with its restricted acres, he had been carried to Chebacco. From Chebacco, he had transferred to South Danvers, and from there to Salem. Now, with wings full-fledged, he was to become a citizen of the capital of Massachusetts, where his great gifts were to be quickly recognized,—and rewarded.

There is an interesting parallel between the careers of Daniel Webster and of his admirer, Rufus Choate. Both were Dartmouth College graduates and early made reputations as orators; both became lawyers, and, after periods of apprenticeship in small villages, settled in Atlantic coast towns, Webster in Portsmouth and Choate in Salem; each moved to Boston at the age of thirty-five, after having served two terms in the national House of Representatives. For a considerable time, each sat in Congress as United States Senator from Massachusetts. Both loved their country passionately and were willing to endure almost any sacrifice in order to preserve its integrity; indeed they suffered obloquy and ostracism because they refused to allow the slavery issue to divide the Union. Each one died, finally, a disappointed man, conscious that the Ship of State was headed towards the rocks.

CHAPTER V

Years of Growth

*A*T the age of thirty-five, with his enthusiasm still aflame, Rufus Choate became a Bostonian, a citizen of no mean city, for Boston was, in those times, of far more importance relatively in the nation than it is to-day. It was also growing rapidly, increasing from 115,000 in 1845 to 160,000 in 1855. It was not the cosmopolitan and polyglot community which we know. The leading citizens were all of Anglo-Saxon lineage, and the people had a racial and cultural unity which was lost in the great tide of immigration before and after the Civil War. The Boston Chamber of Commerce, founded in 1836, was composed of such merchants as Charles and William Amory, the Forbeses, David Sears, William Appleton, Abbot Lawrence, and Samuel Hooper. At dinners on Beacon Street or in Louisburg Square, one might meet Edward Everett or Ralph Waldo Emerson, John Quincy Adams or Josiah Quincy, Caleb Cushing or Daniel Webster. Young men, like Longfellow and Lowell and Holmes and

Dana, were on the road to fame. William Lloyd Garrison was laboriously printing his *Liberator*, and William Hickling Prescott was about to publish his first histories. Horace Mann was opening a new era in education. One might see Charles Bulfinch pausing in front of his masterpiece, the new State House,—a wornout and disappointed man. Boston was indeed, in the 1830's and 1840's, the "Athens of America," if not the "Hub of the Universe."

Choate soon learned to love its crooked streets and narrow alleys. He liked his daily walk around the Common, where half the persons that one met were acquaintances,—for Boston was still more like a large town than a metropolis and there was friendliness in the air. He enjoyed prowling through the bookshelves at the Boston Athenaeum, the quaint library which has been so serviceable to students and writers and which is now more truly "Bostonian" than perhaps any other place in the city. He found the theaters and concert halls diverting. He was proud of the historic spots,— Faneuil Hall and King's Chapel and the Old State House and the Old South Church. But what pleased him most, after all, was the legal atmosphere in which he found himself as soon as he got his bearings.

Choate was, of course, no longer a novice. A man who had served two terms in Congress and had become a leader of the Essex County Bar had nothing to dread in Boston. Nevertheless he had his apprehensions, for he could not be sure how he and his peculiar method of speaking would be received. Naturally the advent of a new and formidable competitor was viewed with interest in State and Court Streets, and his appearance in the Suffolk County Courts made him the object of some close scrutiny. He was to be pitted against lawyers who had already achieved reputations,—men like Samuel Hoar and Leland and Pickering and Farley and Greenleaf, to say nothing of Franklin Dexter and Daniel Webster. It was only a brief period, however, before Choate was moving among them as an equal. His strongly marked individuality was criticized, but it came to be his greatest asset. Soon his fervid eloquence, his vehement gestures, and his brilliant tactics in the courtroom were being discussed in Boston clubs as they had been discussed not long before in Salem, and he became a personage. No one could ever mistake him for any one else. He was always Rufus Choate.

The partnership formed in 1834 between Choate and Benjamin F. Crowninshield lasted fifteen years, during which period no formal division of the office income was ever made, each partner apparently taking what clients he could secure. Even after he had moved to Boston, Choate's cases were, for some months, largely in the Essex County Courts, and he still retained most of his old Salem clients. His first case before the Supreme Court of Middlesex County, held in Cambridge, was for the plaintiff in *Mitchell* v. *Tibbetts*, in January, 1836. In the previous November he had appeared at the Essex County sitting of the Court in several notable cases, arguing against Caleb Cushing in the suit of *The Merchants Bank of Newburyport* v. *Joseph Williams* and losing for his client, the defendant. But it was not long before Boston clients were coming to Choate in such numbers that he actually was obliged to decline cases. He became far more particular as to the criminal business which he undertook, and insisted on a retainer of $100 before he would undertake a defense.

There is ample evidence that Choate's advancement at the Boston Bar was very rapid during the years from 1834 to 1841. With no political duties to hamper him, he could devote himself assiduously to the law, and he was never happier. Occasionally he would prepare and deliver a lecture for the Lyceum stage, but this was for him a diversion, not a task. His real devotion was to his profession. Seldom has any man thrown himself so unreservedly into any occupation. Even after he had retired for the night, the lights were left burning in his study so that, when an idea occurred to his restless mind, he could get up, rush to his desk, and put it down on paper, where it would not fade from his memory. Once he was arguing a case in an interior town and staying at the local tavern. The opposing counsel, waking at two o'clock in the morning, saw a light shining across the corridor in Choate's room, and, apprehensive lest the latter might have been taken ill, went in. There was Choate, fully dressed, his hair standing out in all directions, sitting at a small table and writing energetically. Apologizing for his intrusion, the attorney explained his fears; whereupon Choate replied that, having slept enough, he could not resist getting up and putting in a few hours more in preparation for the next day's ordeal. Who could beat a man like that?

Although he could concentrate amazingly on a case on which he was engaged, he still gained diversion by his reading. "If I could not get any time from my law for liberal and grateful studies," he told Parker, "I'd give up the law from my present case." There were some years during this period when, in the retrospect, he felt that he had perhaps applied himself too exclusively to his practice. "A man is disgusted with law when he is dosed, surfeited," he said. He even admitted that he might have "dried" his mind by too much devotion to his profession. But if he did so, it could have been for only a few years, while he was establishing himself in Boston, and his very refusal to allow himself to be drawn away may account for the position which he attained as a leader of the Boston Bar.

Choate, even in his successes, did not arouse the jealousy of his rival lawyers. He was so free from arrogance and conceit, so courteous to his seniors and so kind to his juniors, that no one could grudge him the place which he had so honestly earned. Of self-seeking and self-praise he was absolutely innocent, and he was generous in his recognition of merit in others. Even when exasperated by stupidity, he never failed to be a gentleman.

Happy in his profession, Choate had put politics from his mind. "No one can do anything in politics of consequence," he said, in one of his reflective moods, "except by making it a deliberate experiment, business, and occupation. If a man does that, he runs all the risks of being thrown over any minute by a fickle and demagogue-blinded people." Quite content with being a lawyer, Choate had abandoned any thought of becoming a statesman. . . . And then, in the winter of 1841, a situation developed which forced him to reconsider his determination of 1834.

Choate's old friend and colleague in Congress, John Davis, had resigned as United States Senator in order to become Governor of Massachusetts, and Choate was

[95]

urged to allow his name to be used as a candidate to fill the vacancy. He resisted the appeal, however, with the result that Isaac C. Bates, another of his former Congressional associates, was nominated by the Whigs and elected by the General Court. The temptation to return to political life seemed to have been evaded. But on February 22, Daniel Webster, not unexpectedly, accepted the offer to become Secretary of State in Harrison's cabinet, and another senatorial opportunity presented itself. Many possible candidates were suggested, including Caleb Cushing, John Quincy Adams, Edward Everett, and others; but Webster himself preferred Choate, and it was soon apparent that public opinion leaned in the same direction, possibly actuated by the diabolical motive of inducing an unwilling victim to accept an office which so many others were not disinclined to grasp.

There were some Whigs who did not altogether approve of Choate, one of them being John Greenleaf Whittier, who wrote to Caleb Cushing:

For myself, I see no reason for the election of Choate. What has he done for the party? What for Massachusetts? He has been acting upon the advice of honest Iago,—"put money in thy purse"; and left thyself and others to peril health, property, & reputation in the long & stern struggle which preceded the late Revolution. And now, forsooth, the old war-tired veterans are to be set aside, to allow this "carpet-knight" to enjoy the spoils.

This judgment on Choate, so completely without understanding of Choate's purpose in withdrawing from active political life, did not appeal to the average voter, who was inclined to respect Choate more for not being a professional office-seeker and who rather liked the idea of having a man of Choate's caliber representing Massachusetts in a body where nearly everybody had some axe to grind or some mission to fulfill. Choate himself was decidedly reluctant to abandon his law practice, even for a few months each year, and it was only under pressure from Webster and others that he yielded. He really could not afford to relinquish the income from his growing clientage; he wanted to be independent in his views on public affairs, not shackled by the fetters of party loyalty; he needed all his leisure hours for the literature which he loved,—and yet he postponed all his cherished projects, including a *History of Greece*, in order to serve the nation. In some men the expressed "Nolo Episcopari" is so clearly hypocritical that its speciousness is detected by everybody; but it is incontrovertible that Rufus Choate would have preferred to remain a private citizen and his own master.

General Harrison, whom Choate had supported by

[97]

his voice and his vote in the picturesque campaign of 1840, died within a month after his inauguration, and Choate was selected to deliver in Faneuil Hall a eulogy upon the deceased President. His reputation as an occasional orator had spread far and wide since he had left Salem, and the historic assembly room was packed with those who wished to hear him. His address was a sincere and effective tribute to a man whose death was an irreparable blow to the hopes of the Whigs, who, flushed with their first national success, had expected to put through under his leadership a coherent political program. "He should be remembered," said Choate, "and we will speak of him to our children, as the *good* President." There was little more which could be said about William Henry Harrison.

Within a few weeks Senator Choate was in Washington attending the special session of Congress which Harrison, before his death, had called at the suggestion of Henry Clay. During that period, brief though it was, the entire political outlook had altered. John Tyler, of Virginia, the new President, although he had been elected Vice President on the Whig ticket, was at heart a States Rights Democrat, not disposed to be dictated to by the autocratic Henry Clay; and the dramatic quarrel between Tyler and Clay, which was to split the Whig Party and ruin its chances for accomplishment, could already be predicted. In this dispute, Choate, like a faithful Whig and conservative son of Massachusetts, stood by Clay, and accordingly favored the protective tariff and the National Bank. But he also did his best to bring about, through some dignified compromise, a reconciliation between Clay and Tyler. He might as well have tried to establish amicable relations between a Dublin Catholic and a Londonderry Protestant.

Among the other members of the Senate when the special session of the Twenty-Seventh Congress opened were Franklin Pierce, of New Hampshire, James Buchanan, of Pennsylvania, Silas Wright, of New York, and Thomas H. Benton, of Missouri, who has chronicled its discussions with a refreshing frankness and a sufficient emphasis on his own part in its proceedings. The Whig majority to begin with was nearly fifty in the House and seven in the Senate, and Clay already had a program prepared for legislation. In his characteristic domineering manner he outlined his plans, little suspecting that, beneath the surface, ideas were concealed which were bound to bring trouble. The troublesome issue which brought affairs to a crisis was the project for the reëstablishment of a United States Bank, an institution which Henry Clay, ever since his unsuccessful controversy with "Old Hickory" in the 1830's, had aimed to revive, if only in revenge on the Democrats.

[99]

First of all, the Independent Treasury Acts of the Van Buren Administration were repealed so that the road was clear. Then came a bill for a National Bank, or Fiscal Institution, planned by Ewing, the Secretary of the Treasury, and supposedly in accord with the scruples of Tyler, who had consistently in the past opposed a National Bank and had been a strong supporter of the rights of the separate states. Senator Rives, of Virginia, proposed an amendment making the consent of each individual state necessary for the introduction of a branch bank within its borders. This amendment Clay vigorously opposed, and then Choate spoke in its favor, not because he doubted the constitutionality of the original measure, but because he deemed it good strategy to conciliate, if possible, the President and others who were honestly in doubt as to its legality in the form first presented.

All "bitter-enders," all advocates of "the whole or nothing," all "one-track minds," will not be favorably impressed by Rufus Choate's attitude. His legal experience had taught him that there is usually something to be said on both sides of most questions. In political matters, he felt that to get most of what you want is far better than to get none. Choate had plenty of aggressiveness, but he could always, through his imagination, put himself in the other man's shoes. So, on this occasion, he made a stirring appeal for compromise. His argument may be briefly summarized as follows: "I do not doubt the power of Congress to establish such a bank and such branch banks anywhere within the limits of the United States, but may it not be unwise to exert this power? By adopting the proposed amendment we are likely to have an effective bank within a few months without breaking up the party. If you adhere to the original bill, I am sure that it cannot be passed. We ought to respect the scruples of those men who disagree with us. We ought not to be averse to concessions. We have resorted to conciliatory measures on larger issues,— slavery, for instance,—and we should do the same on this. I want, for my part, to see the National Bank a popular institution, but it can be made so only by winning for it the approval of a decisive majority."

This speech, so intelligent, so tactful, so thoroughly statesmanlike, illustrates both the strength and the weakness of Choate in politics. Scholar and student that he was, he was more interested in promoting the truth than in gaining his own way. He was not the kind of man to run his head blindly against a stone wall when there was a less craggy route around the obstacle. On matters of morals, Choate could be unyielding enough, but, in political differences of opinion, he saw nothing to be made by obstinacy. When the details of establishing

[101]

a National Bank were being considered, Choate was no man to shout,

> Come one, come all. This rock shall fly
> From its firm base as soon as I!

All this is merely saying that Choate was Lincolnian rather than Wilsonian in his idealism.

The arrogant Henry Clay, who, despite his title of the "Great Compromiser," had really little pliability of mind, clashed with Choate in the course of the debate. During Choate's speech, Clay, who was sitting in the next row, interrupted him to ask how Choate had secured his information that the Bank Bill would be vetoed unless it were amended,—the implication being that Choate was in the confidence of the President. Choate, who had really gained his knowledge from Webster, saw no necessity for bringing the name of the Secretary of State into the controversy, and evaded the inquiry. When he had finished, Senator Archer, of Virginia, expressed regret that Clay had attempted to draw from Choate the opinions of the Executive. In the sharp discussion which ensued, Clay rudely broke in on Choate, saying, "That, sir, is not the thing. Did you not say that you could not, without breach of privilege and violation of parliamentary rules, disclose your authority?" "Sir," replied Choate, with more fire than he ordinarily showed on the floor of the Senate, "I insist on my right to explain what I did say in my own words." "I desire a direct answer," continued Clay, in his insolent and overbearing manner. "The gentleman," responded Choate, turning to the President of the Senate, "will have to take the answer as I choose to give it to him." Rufus Choate, of Massachusetts, had no intention of quailing before the autocratic Senator from Kentucky.

Towards those who did not cringe before him, Clay was likely to be courteous. When he discovered that Choate, although a new member, was quite competent to take care of himself in debate, he altered his tactics, and, on the following day, made a handsome apology, disclaiming utterly any intention of placing Choate in an embarrassing position. Never one to refuse a friendly hand, Choate walked around the Hall to Clay's desk and went through the outward form of reconciliation, while the Senators applauded. It was an affair of which Choate had no reason to be ashamed.

In the end, furthermore, Choate was proved to be right. Tyler vetoed the bill for a "Fiscal Bank," and it was impossible to pass the measure over his disapproval. A new act was prepared, still, however, ignoring the President's chief objection,—that the question of the concurrence of the states was left unsettled. Although this passed both houses, Tyler,—who was absolutely consistent in his position,—again interposed his veto. Ultimately all of Tyler's cabinet except Webster resigned, and a new cabinet was appointed, more in sympathy with the President's point of view. The consequence of Clay's obstinacy was that the Whig party was divided and that he had no National Bank of any kind.

Choate's first speech on the Senate floor was made on another subject,—the policy of Webster, as Secretary of State, towards Great Britain in the notorious case of Alexander McLeod. McLeod, a British citizen, had boasted publicly, during a trip into New York State, of his complicity in the capture and burning of the steamer *Caroline* on December 30, 1837, in the Niagara River, when an American had been killed. He was promptly arrested by the authorities and placed in jail; whereupon the British Government, assuming all responsibility for the deeds of McLeod, demanded his release in language which was decidedly threatening. There was uncontrolled excitement for a few weeks, and it actually seemed as if war might result. The incident is one of the most convincing illustrations in history of the need of a Court of Arbitration. Two great and proud countries were on the verge of armed conflict over a matter which, in the private relationships between man and man, would have been settled before a judge or jury. Webster, inheriting the dispute when he took over the Department of State, sent Attorney General Crittenden to observe the trial in the New York courts and render whatever assistance was required. Several Democratic Senators, including Benton, Buchanan, and Calhoun, denounced the administration for its timidity. Choate then rose in defense of Webster, as one friend for another. He made an excellent impression, and Buchanan, in replying, said of him, "Judging of others by myself, I must say that those who have listened to him once will be anxious to hear him again." Sumner, writing Dr. Lieber in June, said,—"Choate will be glad to renew his acquaintance with you; his speech on McLeod's case is masterly." The affair, like a blaze of straw, soon died down. After a change of venue from Niagara County to Oneida County, McLeod was acquitted, and all the noise was quieted. The value of time and good sense in international disputes was never more forcibly demonstrated.

During the same session Choate had an opportunity to appear in behalf of another friend. Defeated in 1839 in his campaign for a fifth term as Governor of Massachusetts, Edward Everett had gone abroad in 1840, and, in the summer of 1841, had been nominated

[105]

by Tyler as Minister to England. No fair-minded person questioned his qualifications for the position. He was both a scholar and a gentleman, endowed with the tact and dignity to represent our country at a moment when there were serious causes for dissension between us and Great Britain. But Everett had declared himself publicly as favoring the immediate abolition of slavery in the District of Columbia, and certain fiery Southerners saw fit to oppose his confirmation on the ground that he was an abolitionist. The debate in a secret session of the Senate was never officially reported, but it was very heated. Both Senator Buchanan and Senator King made savage attacks on Everett. Choate, who was fond of Everett and, like him, deplored the needless agitation of the slavery question, was much aroused, and, with a readiness which astonished those who were not aware of his resourcefulness and power of extemporaneous speech, appealed for a ratification of the nomination. His argument was declared by those who heard it to be "one of the most brilliant and eloquent ever delivered within the walls of the Senate Chamber." During the violent discussion which ensued, Choate wrote Charles Sumner:

Yes, Everett's is a good appointment. Ask me when I get home, *if we did not come near losing him in the Senate*

[106]

from Abolitionism; entre nous,—if we do, then the Union goes to pieces like a potter's vessel.

In those days, predictions of the impending dissolution of the Union were almost as frequent as prophecies about the weather, but they were obviously sincere. Rufus Choate himself, like Webster and Everett, was no apologist for negro slavery; but, like them and many other conservative and law-abiding thinkers of that generation, he disliked extremists from either North or South. He feared that the noisy and irritating attacks of fanatical abolitionists might endanger the Union,—and, for the moment, he believed that the Union was of chief consideration. He was equally concerned lest the open advocates of slavery try to force their opinions upon the North. Fortunately for his apprehensions in this case, Everett was confirmed by the close vote of 23 to 19.

The stormy special session had adjourned in mid-September, and in December Choate was back in Washington, for the opening of the regular session. One of the important issues concerned a bill for providing further remedial justice in the courts of the United States,—a measure designed to cover a situation like the McLeod trial, in which New York State might conceivably, because of a decision rendered in one of its

[107]

courts, have involved the entire nation in a bloody conflict with a foreign power. The proposed measure introduced a fundamental principle,—the right of the
national tribunals to have properly qualified jurisdiction
over criminal causes commenced in state courts and
under state authority. Settling, as it aimed to do, some
of the controverted questions between state and national
jurisdiction, the bill revived the mooted problem of
state rights. Choate's speech favoring the proposed
legislation was delivered in May, 1842, and, as printed
in Brown's *Rufus Choate*, covered nearly fifty pages.
Its argument, which was evidently in some degree
affected by Webster's *Reply to Hayne*, is strong in its
reasoning and is supported in true legal fashion by
ample precedents from court decisions; but it has also
its "purple patches," in which Choate allows his imagination to break free from the restraint of his logic.
The closing passage will, perhaps, illustrate the sweep
of his fancy:

The aspect which our united America turns upon foreign
nations, the aspect which the Constitution designs she shall
turn on them, the guardian of our honor, the guardian of our
peace, is, after all, her grandest and fairest aspect. We have
a right to be proud when we think of that. Happy and free
empress mother of states themselves free, unagitated by the
passions, unmoved by the dissensions of any one of them, she

watches the rights and fame of all, and reposing, secure and serene, along the mountain summits of her freedom, she holds in one hand the fair olive branch of peace, and in the other the thunderbolt and meteor flag of reluctant and rightful war. There may she sit forever,—the stars of union upon her brow, the rock of independence beneath her feet!

Spoken as it was with passion and sincerity, this outburst thrilled the audience in the Senate Chamber. To us, who read the words in cold type, it may seem flamboyant and overdone, like a rococo style of room decoration. But it must be remembered, if we are to be absolutely just, that Choate was the voice of a period of national exuberance and self-consciousness, when statesmen were promulgating the doctrine of "Manifest Destiny" and respectable citizens were shouting "Fifty-four Forty or Fight!" It was a time when the American eagle sometimes screamed defiantly at the whole world and when the favorite pastime of cross-roads orators was twisting the British lion's tail. Even Choate, who had classical standards of good taste, was guilty, under emotional stress, of sentences which bring a smile to the lips of twentieth century critics. But in spite of what seems to be artificiality, they were honest utterances, and we can applaud their spirit and intention even when we deplore their somewhat extravagant verbiage. Perhaps if we could have heard the words as Choate delivered them, with his fervent patriotism glowing in his splendid eyes, we should be less inclined to dwell upon their faults. And, from a practical point of view, the speech was successful, for the Remedial Justice Bill was passed early in July.

Meanwhile, during the late spring and early summer of 1842, Webster and Lord Ashburton were busy framing the treaty which bears the latter's name. It was submitted on August 11 to the Senate, where it was warmly debated in secret session, Benton and Buchanan being very vigorous in opposition to it. Here again Choate came to Webster's assistance, defending the Treaty skilfully against its critics. Much to Choate's satisfaction, it was ratified on August 20 by a decisive vote. While he was thoroughly patriotic, he was in full accord with any policy which would adjust honorably and peaceably the differences between the Anglo-Saxon peoples. His good sense led him to avoid the chauvinistic Anglophobia which animated so many Jefferson Bricks in the 1840's.

There are probably few subjects in all the scope of American politics less romantic than the tariff. New England manufacturers fought bitterly then as they do to-day for duties which would increase their profits and reduce competition, but the average consumer's heart is not likely to beat faster as he glances through arguments for protection. Rufus Choate was Senator from a state the large industries of which were dependent,—or thought they were dependent,—on the protective system. Hence we find him, in two long speeches,—one on March 14, 1842, and the other on April 12 and 15, 1844,—developing a coherent philosophy of industrialism. In the first, he devotes himself mainly to proving that Congress has the Constitutional power to establish protective duties, or, as he puts it, "to provide for the collection of the necessary revenues of government, so as to afford reasonable and adequate protection to the whole labor of the country, agricultural, navigating, mechanical, and manufacturing." To-day it would be deemed a waste of time to dwell on so obvious a doctrine; yet Choate, to make his demonstration convincing, covered the entire field of Constitutional history, with a wealth of illustration and quotation worthy of an argument before the Supreme Court of the United States.

In April, 1844, in connection with a bill of Senator McDuffie's proposing to revive the so-called Compromise Tariff Act of 1838, Choate refused to admit that there could be any doubt as to the wisdom of a protective tariff, and maintained that "it would be supreme madness, worthy only of a government nodding to its fall, to overturn it." This speech, covering nearly seventy-five

[111]

pages, is a scholarly document filled with statistics and technical details, opening with a discussion of the debates of the First Congress, from which he drew the conclusion that the earliest tariff bill under the Constitution, passed on July 4, 1789, was based on the principle of protection:

It sought to bring such a sum of money into the Treasury as the wants of administration exacted; but it sought to effect this by such arrangements of detail, by such discriminations of high and low duties, by prohibition here, by total exemption there, as should secure to the vast and various labor of America, on the land, in the shop, on the sea, a clear and adequate advantage over the labor of the alien nations of the world.

His argument, however, was not all facts and figures. From time to time, with consummate skill, he paused as if to enrich his logic with sentiment. Pointing out that the statesmen of 1816, disgusted with the commercial theories of Jefferson, had turned to the building of a sound protective tariff, he added, as if in an afterthought:

Foul shame they deemed it that the American soldier at least should not sleep under an American blanket; that the very halyards by which we send up the stars and stripes in the hour of naval battle should be made in a Russian ropewalk;

that an American frigate should ride at anchor by a British chain cable.

This kind of doctrine was greatly relished by "the solid men of Boston," and we may be sure that they were not displeased when Choate, in concluding his long address, spoke feelingly regarding Massachusetts, insisting that she had a right to her views on great questions:

Permit me to say that you must take the States of America as you find them. All of them have their peculiarities. All have their traits. . . . South Carolina has hers. Massachusetts has hers. She will continue to think, speak, print, just what she pleases, on every subject that may interest the patriot, the moralist, the Christian. But she will be true to the Constitution.

It was during the sharp debate which followed this speech that McDuffie, the morose and irritable South Carolina Senator who had been wounded more than once in personal encounters, denounced Choate with characteristic insolence; whereupon Choate, who feared no man alive, replied in language for him unusually bitter, outdoing the Southern fire-eater in vituperation and keeping the Senate convulsed with laughter at his lambent wit. The victory was so obviously with Choate

[113]

that McDuffie did not even resort to his customary final argument,—a challenge to a duel.

Another subject upon which Choate had something to say during his term as Senator was the matter of Oregon Territory. Conventions in 1818 and 1837 between Great Britain and the United States had arranged for the joint occupation of this disputed section by "the vessels, citizens, and subjects of the two powers." The increasing emigration of American pioneers to the Northwest, however, created new problems; and, when our settlers asked for protection against the Hudson's Bay Company, Senator Linn, of Missouri, brought in a bill providing for a chain of blockhouses across the continent and for grants of land to those who would take the journey. This measure precipitated an acrimonious discussion early in the third session of the Twenty-Seventh Congress, which assembled on December 5, 1842. Although Jeremiah Mason had written Webster in late August, "It is generally understood that Mr. Choate will resign at the end of this session," Choate had decided to retain his seat, and found himself assigned to places on the Committee on Naval Affairs, the Committee on the Library, and the Committee on Foreign Relations.

When Linn's bill was being considered in January, 1843, Choate declared that, while he approved in gen-

Rufus Choate, from the Portrait in the Possession of Charles F. Choate, III

eral of the theory behind it, the provision making a grant of lands to settlers was, in his opinion, contrary to the spirit of the agreement with Great Britain. In a speech a few days later, Choate argued for two hours in defense of the Ashburton Treaty, asserting that in it the United States had had "immeasurably the best of the bargain." Benton and Choate, who were not temperamentally or politically in accord, had a spirited controversy over the Northwestern boundary line, in which maps and treaties were introduced as evidence. Choate spoke again on February 2, endeavoring to prove that the boundary intended by the Treaty of 1783 was the one adopted by the Ashburton Treaty in 1842. The bill was finally passed on that afternoon, 24 to 22, Choate voting, of course, in the negative.

In January, 1844, Senator Semple, of Illinois, introduced a resolution asking the President to give notice to the British Government of our desire to end the joint occupation agreement under the Convention of 1827. While the measure was being debated, Choate spoke twice: on February 22, in reply to Atchison, of Missouri; and on March 21, in summing up the arguments. The latter speech, which was fully reported, was a statesmanlike utterance, urging the Senate not unnecessarily to antagonize Great Britain. Choate's chief objection was that Semple's proposal would embarrass the

[115]

Department of State during the negotiations then being carried on with England, and he did not hesitate to express his frank disapprobation of those Americans who were stirring up bad feeling between the two great nations. His words on this topic are applicable to-day:

> Let me say that, in my judgment, this notion of a national enmity of feeling towards Great Britain belongs to a past age of our history. My younger countrymen are unconscious of it. They disavow it. . . . We are born to happier feelings. We look on England as we look on France. . . . If public men, or any one public man, think it their duty to make a war or cultivate the dispositions of war towards any nation, let them perform the duty, and have done with it. But I do say that there is an unfortunate, morbid, impracticable popular temper on the subject, which you desire to resist, but are afraid you shall not be able to resist. If you will answer for the politicians, I think I will venture to answer for the people.

This is the kind of wisdom which wins our admiration. Choate was surrounded in the Senate by Anglophobes and expansionists and jingoes, all of whom would have welcomed war, convinced as they were that the United States could defeat any nation on earth. That he could, in the midst of this turmoil, keep his wits about him and raise his voice in favor of abstract justice shows that he was a far-sighted statesman.

In the winter of 1843-44, Choate reiterated his

[116]

intention of resigning, and gossip in Boston set March 1, 1844, as the date when he planned to withdraw from the Senate. Suggestions were made to Webster that he allow himself to be chosen in Choate's place. But Webster, after giving the proposal careful consideration, decided that it would not be worth his while to go back to the Senate for the brief period still remaining of Choate's term. Choate then resolved, in spite of his distaste for public life, to stick it out for the remaining months.

In his final session, Choate's most important efforts in debate were given to the momentous question of Texas. A Treaty of Annexation, negotiated by Calhoun, as Secretary of State, had been signed on April 12, 1844, but it was impossible to secure the two-thirds vote necessary in the Senate for ratification. In the Presidential campaign which followed, Polk, a Democrat and an annexationist, defeated Henry Clay, who had vacillated in his views on the subject of Texas. Convinced that the Democrats had a mandate from the people, President Tyler called upon Congress to arrange by joint resolution for the annexation of Texas,—a procedure which required only a majority vote in both Houses. It was a clever scheme, and Congress proceeded to carry through the plan.

In February, 1845, after the joint resolutions had

[117]

passed the House, they were considered by the Senate, where nearly every member expressed his opinion. On February 18, Choate spoke for three hours. Unfortunately this speech was not reported in full, only a summary being printed in the *Congressional Globe*. He began by stating that, in his opinion, Congress had no power whatever to pass a resolution of this kind and that such action, no matter what good would be derived from it, would be unconstitutional. He pointed out that the power to admit new states was clearly not intended to imply the right to annex foreign governments. He dwelt at some length on the devious strategy of the Democrats, who, defeated in the attempts to secure a legitimate two-thirds vote in the Senate, had resorted to an unusual method which required only a majority in each House. "We could not," he continued, "admit Texas by joint resolution even if it would ensure a thousand years of liberty to the Union. If, like the fabled garden of old, its rivers should run pearls, and its trees bear imperial fruit of gold,—yet even then we could not admit her, because it would be a sin against the Constitution." After this characteristic exaggeration, he went on to say that, even if this extraordinary procedure were technically constitutional, it would still be inexpedient. It would be an unwise policy, sure to recoil dangerously upon the nation at a later period.

Choate's protests, although eloquently presented, were futile. The gods were on the side of his opponents, and the joint resolution eventually passed the Senate by the close vote of 27 to 25, with Bates and Choate, the Massachusetts Senators, standing fast in the minority. In the light of future history, it is undoubtedly fortunate that Choate and his friends did not succeed in blocking the joint resolution. Hazardous as it looked to them in 1845, the annexation of Texas was an essential step in our national development. Choate's opposition was based, not so much on sound statesmanship as on sectional prejudice,—the fear that the South might gain the preponderance in the Union. We can recognize that his apprehensions were groundless, but the truth was not so clear before Gettysburg and Appomattox had settled the issue for decades to come.

During this last session in the Senate, Choate spoke much more frequently than he had done before. When a bill was introduced providing for the joint admission of the territories of Florida and Iowa into the Union, Choate objected, insisting that each state should be admitted separately. The basis of his opposition was the fact that the Constitution of Florida contained two obnoxious clauses, one prohibiting the emancipation of slaves and the other forbidding the introduction of free negroes into the state. Once again Choate's voice was

[119]

raised unsuccessfully, and the measure was passed by a large majority.

Much more constructive were Choate's activities in connection with the Smithsonian Institution. The money bequeathed by James Smithson to the United States Government,—amounting to more than half a million dollars,—was received in 1838, and there were widely differing opinions as to what should be done with it. Senator Tappan, of Ohio, introduced, in December, 1844, a measure providing for the selection of grounds, the erection of buildings, and the appointment of professors and lecturers in scientific subjects, including chemistry, geology, and astronomy, as well as agriculture and horticulture. A few weeks later Choate expressed himself as opposed to the plan for a university and offered an amendment appropriating a sum of not less than twenty thousand dollars each year for the purchase of books and manuscripts. On this occasion he made an appeal for the establishment in the United States of a national library second to none in Europe, and deplored the fact that not a library in our country then included more than fifty thousand volumes. This speech was said by one who heard it to be "the most beautiful that ever fell from human lips"; and Calhoun, who stood near, leaning on the back of a chair, exclaimed to those near him, "Massachusetts sent us a

Webster, but, in the name of heaven, whom have they sent us now?" Amended as Choate desired, the bill passed the Senate on January 23, but it could not be put through the House until the next session, when Choate was no longer in Congress. It became a law in August, 1846, and Rufus Choate was elected a member of the Board of Regents of the Smithsonian Institution. In its final form the appropriation was to be devoted entirely to the purposes of a library.

Although the policy of the Institution might now have been considered as settled, the Board of Regents were divided, many of them preferring what was called "a system of active operations." In the end, the party devoted to the promotion of science came to dominate, and the library fell into a subordinate position. When Choate discovered the situation, he resigned, in January, 1855, as Regent, declaring himself not in harmony with the aims of his fellow members. Fortunately his desire for a great library in the capital of the New World, "into which shall be slowly, but surely and judiciously, gathered the best thoughts of all the civilizations," was gratified with the creation of the Congressional Library, which represents to-day what he was trying to obtain more than three-quarters of a century ago.

On March 3, 1845, the Senate assembled for the

[121]

closing day of the session. Some miscellaneous matters came up for discussion, including Oregon, Indian Appropriations, Naturalization and Election Frauds, Navy and Army Appropriations, and Harbors. The Senate authorized the President to sell two Arabian horses presented to an American Consul by the Imaum of Muscat. Some pension bills brought over from the House of Representatives were perfunctorily passed. Senator Magnum, the Presiding Officer, thanked the Senate for its courtesy to him, and the body adjourned at half-past two in the morning,—*sine die*. The reign of John Tyler, of Virginia, was almost over. The triumphant Democracy, having overwhelmed the Whigs and Henry Clay, was once more in the saddle. As for Rufus Choate, he had cast his last vote in the Senate of the United States, or in any legislative body. Daniel Webster, whose place he had taken in 1841, was elected to succeed him; and Choate went back to his clients and his library, where he could be completely at ease. "If I could be permanently and happily in the Senate," he told Parker, "I should like that better than anything in the world; but to be just enough in the Senate to be out of the law, and not enough in the Senate to be a leader in politics, is a sort of half-and-half business very contemptible." From this time on his sole mistress was the law, and politics had only an incidental and minor place in his career.

[122]

CHAPTER VI

A Comprehensive Mind

*T*HERE were certain periods in Choate's life when he was a living refutation of the theory that a man, to be successful, must give himself exclusively to his profession. Nothing about him is more remarkable than his ability to ride several horses,—law, literature, lecturing, and politics,—at once, without stumbling or slipping off any one of them. When Parker told him how much he was liking the law, Choate said, "Of course I like it! There's nothing else for any man of intellect to like. Politics is shifting, unsteady, and capricious, and doesn't satisfy the intellect." Outlining his philosophy in 1855, he declared, "It is well enough for an American, at some portion of his life, to go into Congress for a brief time, if opportunity offers, as a sort of recreation and for pleasurable observation; but the *great aim* of a young man should be advocacy." And yet he also admitted that a mind confined solely to the law is narrow, and not of a high order. "Five hours a day, including practice," he added, "is enough for the law."

[123]

In conversation he confessed that "the study of law, like the study of any severe abstract science, takes a man out of connection with the common thoughts of man, and out of sympathy with the common heart." It was, perhaps, because of his other varied pursuits,—his interest in literature, in public speaking, and in governmental problems,—that Rufus Choate became the supreme advocate that he was.

He had never, even when most engrossed in Senate affairs, forgotten that he was a lawyer by preference and profession. His initial appearance before the Supreme Court of the United States was made in a patent case, *Prouty* v. *Ruggles*, in 1842, Choate being for the plaintiffs and the distinguished Massachusetts attorney, Franklin Dexter, for the defendants. Suit had been brought for the recovery of damages for an alleged infringement of a patent obtained by the plaintiffs for an improvement in the construction of a plow. In the original trial the jury gave a verdict for the defendants, and this decision was sustained by the Supreme Court. Thus he lost his first case before the highest judicial body in the country. It took more than one failure, however, to injure Choate's reputation. Charles Sumner expressed the general feeling when he wrote in February, 1842, from Boston, regarding Choate,—"His position here is very firm. He is the leader of our bar, with an overwhelming superfluity of business, with a strong taste for books and learned men, with great amiableness of character, with uncommon eloquence and untiring industry."

After Congress adjourned on March 3, 1843, Choate returned at once to Boston, where he kept for some weeks what he called "an imperfect journal of readings and actions." Like most diaries of this sort, it was not continued for any long period; yet it throws much light on his ideals and on his manner of work. The Puritan in him was constantly urging him towards self-improvement. After recording his desire to be a "student of professional forensic rhetoric," he concludes that "careful constant writing is the parent of ripe speech." "I have long been in the practice," he wrote, "of reading daily some first class English writer, chiefly for the *copia verborum*, to avoid sinking into cheap and bald fluency, to give elevation, energy, sonorousness, and refinement, to my vocabulary." It was for practical reasons that he steeped himself in Demosthenes and Quintilian and Burke, trying to discover the secret of their mastery of words. . . . But he could also read for delight, with no further ulterior motive. On May 17, he prepares his argument in the important case of the Ipswich Manufacturing Company, but finds relaxation and refreshment in the fifth book of the *Odyssey*, in the lines which describe "the extorted, unanticipated, and mysterious communication,—unanticipated by, and mysterious to him,—of Calypso to Ulysses on the seashore, in which she bids him dry his tears, and cease to consume his life." Doubtless Homer's marvelous dactyls did not assist Choate in his legal labors, but they did help him to feed his hungry soul.

In one week he reads and summarizes sections of *Greenleaf On Evidence* and of *Story on the Dissolution of Partnership;* he discusses some of the "pregnant pages" of Tacitus; he finishes Johnson's *Lives,* as far as that of Dryden; he relaxes with *Antony and Cleopatra,*—marking, however, any felicity or available peculiarity of phrase,—and then stiffens himself with Quintilian's chapters on *Writing* and on *Extempore Speech.* On June 24, he mentions "a most happy method of legal study, by which I believe and feel that I am reviving my love of the law,"—a procedure which he gives for our delectation:

I have adopted the plan of taking a volume, the last volume of Massachusetts Reports, and of making a full brief of an argument on every question in every case, examining all the authorities, finding others, and carefully composing an argument as well reasoned, as well expressed as if I were going to submit it to a bench of the first of jurists.

[126]

Surely this is an astounding practice for a Senator of the United States, almost forty-five years of age, standing at the pinnacle of his profession! It illustrates the thoroughness with which he kept himself prepared for every emergency, just as a champion athlete keeps himself in training by exercise. But it is even more amazing to find him noting that, on the same day, he read the Temptation in *Matthew*, *Mark*, and *Luke*, in the original Greek, and then what he describes as "that grand and grave poem which Milton has built upon those few and awful verses, *Paradise Regained*." The transition from a volume of Massachusetts *Reports* to Milton's noble epic seems to him to be entirely natural.

There were other interests for Rufus Choate besides politics and legal studies and the reading of the classics, —he was also becoming well known as a platform orator. At the close of this memorable year of labor, on December 22, 1843, he delivered in the old Broadway Tabernacle, the largest auditorium in New York City, a lecture before the New England Association, the subject being *The Age of the Pilgrims the Heroic Period of Our History*. It was a great occasion, for the hall was full and Daniel Webster and other distinguished men were on the platform. Choate, then in the prime of life, dealing with a topic which aroused his sympathies and stimulated his emotions, thrilled the

[127]

audience with the splendor of his periods. With inimitable skill, he sketched the conditions and the elements which must meet to produce a heroic time and an heroic race; he portrayed the English Puritan character and traced the history of Puritanism, pausing to dwell with particular stress on the residence of certain exiled Puritans, during the reign of "Bloody Mary," at Geneva, in a country where, to their lasting benefit, they found "an independent, peaceful, law-abiding, well-governed, and prosperous commonwealth."

There was a state without king or nobles; there was a church without a bishop; there was a people governed by grave magistrates which it had selected, and equal laws which it had framed.

This paragraph, it is said, was received with a burst of applause such as had never been heard within the walls of the Tabernacle. Choate was so amazed by the enthusiasm that he turned to Dr. William Adams, who was sitting at his side, to ask for an explanation. He had never been greeted in such a way before.

He went on, in his rich and sonorous baritone, to show that the Puritans had certain strongly marked traits: a sense of religious duty; a thirst for freedom,— "freedom of the soul, freedom of thought, a larger measure of freedom of life"; a capacity for enduring privation and hardship, without the sustaining aid of anybody but themselves. It was this last quality that marked their finest heroism,—that alone, with no spectators to look on and applaud, and unstained by the ordinary passions, aims, stimulants, and excitations of life, they battled with loneliness and famine and disease, and finally, with a glorious gesture, sent back the *Mayflower*, and, after that pitiless winter on the Cape, remained behind among the graves of their dead and their hopes for the future. As he approached the climax, the audience was irresistibly moved. Webster's eyes filled with tears, and his great frame shook, and he bowed his head to conceal his emotion. . . . And then Choate closed in subdued tones, like a gray evening after a gaudy day.

I have dwelt at some length on this oration because, in its style and its delivery, it was the product of Choate's systematic study of ancient and modern eloquence. While he was practising law and attending to routine business,—of which he had no small amount, —he was also spending an hour or two a day in an examination of Cicero and Burke, becoming familiar with the "matter and manner" of these masters of speech. Choate's apparent spontaneity was invariably the result of careful planning. He sets himself the task of going through the oration of Demosthenes *On*

[129]

the Crown,—"which I will completely master, translate, annotate, and commit." He concludes that Burke is the fourth Englishman,—Shakspere, Bacon, Milton, Burke,"—and praises him for his "marvelous English, universal wisdom, illuminated, omniscient mind." And all the while he was trying to see how he could emulate these speakers in their oratorical virtues.

In the summer of 1844, after a busy Congressional session, he reached Boston, eager to "reconstruct" his life at home and to regain what he had lost in spending so many hours among politicians.

I must revive and advance the faded memory of the law; and I can devise no better method than that of last summer,— the preparation of a careful brief, on every case in Metcalf's last volume, of an argument in support of the decision. In preparing this brief, law, logic, eloquence, must be studied and blended together. The airy phrase, the turn of real reply, are to be sought and written out.

He translates the Catilinian Orations, reads and ponders on the *Odyssey*, starts to write "the history of the formation and adoption of the Constitution." He announces that "style and manner are to be assiduously cultivated and carefully adapted to the subject." Later in the summer he turns, after a rereading of Tacitus,

[130]

to a study of modern European history. Disgusted with his waste of profitable hours, he makes a vow:

I have gone through a week of unusual labor; not wholly satisfactory to myself. I deliberately record my determination to make no more political speeches, and to take no more active part in the election or in practical politics. . . . I have earned the discharge. . . . To my profession, *totis viribus*, I am now dedicated. To my profession of the law and of advocacy, with as large and fair an accompaniment of manly and graceful studies as I can command.

No man of his distinction and achievement could expect to keep out of political life. Within a few weeks after his emphatic declaration, he is found making a campaign appeal to the Boston Whigs, boasting that they would "*return* James K. Polk to the Convention that *discovered* him." Predicting Polk's defeat by Clay, he declared that the former would "disappear like the lost Pleiad, where no telescope could find him!" It was an unfortunate prophecy, and was not to be fulfilled. Until the contest was over, however, Choate gave valuable hours to speeches in behalf of Henry Clay, addressing great throngs at Concord, Springfield, and Lynn, and denouncing vehemently the annexation of Texas.

When the fight was settled and the Democrats were

[131]

manifestly victorious, Choate set out once more for Washington, resolved to close "in two months, forever, my political life."

In the capital during that session of 1844-45 his usual day began with an hour's walk before breakfast, followed by the reading of the morning paper and of a few pages from Johnson or Milton,—after which he had a light meal. He then conscientiously prepared himself for his Senatorial duties, answered correspondence, and gave an hour or two to some of his law cases before the Supreme Court. Next came the Senate session itself, at which he was to be found regularly in his seat, for he had a scrupulous regard for his legislative duties. . . . But even with all these routine obligations to meet, he was in a few weeks deep in Thucydides, so deep that he soon had built an outline for a comprehensive work on the history and culture of ancient Greece. "To approach to the accomplishment of this design," he wrote, "it must be my only literary labor,— my only labor not professional. It may well, and it positively must, supersede all others." This plan was for many years in the back of his mind, and he never abandoned it until Grote's history made any similar book superfluous.

When he could cast off the mantle of his office, he felt himself relieved of a chafing burden. Putting down in his *Diary* the words, "The session ended. Boston, March 10, 1845," he wrote:

To resume my ante-Homeric Greece, I have but to procure a Niebuhr and Muller in addition to books already at hand, to review the collections accumulated at Washington, and begin. But all this is to be held in strictest subordination to law and to business. It is to be relaxation and recreation strictly, yet is it to improve style, reason, taste, and habits of research.

He was free at last from his shackles,—free to bury himself in his books and to spend long hours on the work which he loved best. And yet it is probable that he had no real regrets for the time which he had spent in politics. In his conversation, he could not refrain from being cynical on the subject. "It's a curious whimsicality of the people," he said, "that if a man by fortune and character is finely fitted for public life, they won't take him. As soon as a man has been three years in Congress, the people grow impatient of him. There seems to be something in the taste of northern society which forbids permanency in public life. . . ." But, despite these caustic comments, Choate demonstrated in his own case that political training helps to liberalize a lawyer's mind. He had profited by his experience. He had learned to know the great men of the

[133]

country; he had acquired a national rather than a provincial point of view; he had measured himself, not without success, against the finest intellects of that generation. When he settled down in Boston once more, he was a citizen, not of Essex County, or even of Massachusetts, but of the United States.

CHAPTER VII

The Great Advocate

*M*ANY acute and discriminating critics who knew Rufus Choate in the full maturity of his powers have agreed that he was the most eminent American lawyer not only of his own time but of any time. To prove this is as difficult as it is to prove that Garrick was greater than John Barrymore or Jenny Lind more exquisite than Galli Curci. But judging by the impression which Choate made on those who heard him, his superior in a courtroom trial has not appeared on our continent. Professor Greenleaf, a well-known legal writer, once described Choate as *"more terrible* than Webster," and even the ablest attorneys in Boston dreaded to oppose him. "What's the use of my going on term after term fighting cases for corporations, with Choate to close on me for the plaintiff?" asked one of them. "If I have fifty cases, I shan't gain a single one."

For some years Choate's law office was located at 4 Court Street, an entry famous for the influential men who had quarters there. On the same floor with Choate

[135]

were Charles Sumner, George S. Hillard, Theophilus Parsons, and John A. Andrew, later War Governor of Massachusetts. On the floor above were Horace Mann, the educational reformer, Edward C. Loring, and Luther Stearns Cushing, the author of Cushing's *Manual*. Choate and Crowninshield had two rooms,—one for the clerks and one for Choate's inner sanctum. There was none of the elaborate mechanism, the smart looking secretaries and formal atmosphere which one finds on State Street to-day. The central feature of Choate's office equipment was a high stand-up desk which had once belonged to Judge William H. Prescott, —father of the historian,—in Salem, in front of which was a chair of peculiar shape so made that a person could slightly sit upon it while still remaining on his feet. Here he usually stood, pen in hand, hard at work, with rows of pigeon holes in front of him filled with legal papers. In the center of the room was a table, at which, however, Choate seldom sat, preferring either to lean at his desk or to recline upon the haircloth sofa in the corner. The place was littered with books, official blanks, legal documents, and other dry looking reading matter, arranged with no particular system. After the old carpet was worn out, Choate asked his young associate, Parker, to "indicate what kind of a new one he desired." When Parker suggested an oilcloth,

Choate, who always dreaded a chill, replied, "Oh, no, that's too cold a material. I'd rather walk on marble than on oilcloth." In the end Choate left the decision to the colored woman who cleaned the office, and she produced a carpet of flaming red, much to the occupant's satisfaction,—for red was his favorite color.

When he was not away or engaged in court, Choate came regularly to his office, even in the roughest weather. Often when he was too ill to stand up, he would lie on the sofa and advise his clients. In January, 1849, when he took a new partner, Joseph Mills Bell, who later became his son-in-law, the office was moved to 7½ Tremont Row, but the familiar yellow pine desk was taken along, as well as most of the other furniture, and Choate continued his earlier habits. Filing cabinets were then unknown, but he could usually put his hand at once on what was wanted. Choate was invariably cheerful and good-natured, even when he was ill or when things were in confusion. Everybody, down to the man who carried out the ashes, received from him a kindly salutation.

In his early days in Boston, Choate was careless in making out his accounts and often set his charges ridiculously low. As a consequence, he accumulated very little property. He himself was indifferent to money, but after 1849, when the new firm was formed,

[137]

the system was changed. Bell, his partner, now put his fees on a more rational scale, with the result that the average annual receipts of the office from 1849 to 1859, while Choate was engaged in about seventy cases a year, were not far from $18,000. In 1856, his most profitable year, he took in more than $22,000. The largest fee accepted by Choate was $2,500,—a sum which he received in only four instances. He once was given a retaining fee of $1,500. Nathan Crosby told the story of being in Choate's office when a client asked what his bill would be for a written opinion upon a matter of importance. "Hand me one hundred dollars, and I will sign a receipt in full," said Choate. "If you go to my partner in the other room who keeps the books, he will make you pay one hundred and fifty sure." A young lawyer who had engaged Choate as his senior handed him $50, remarking that he believed it was the amount the latter had asked for a retainer. "No," replied Choate, "I named $25, but you said $50, and I *yielded*."

For his own part, he never bothered with accounts. He once planned to start a system of double-entry bookkeeping, actually purchasing the ledger and putting down one item, "Office debtor one gallon of oil." This, however, was the sole entry that was ever made. It was only during his last decade, when his partner watched

[138]

over his finances, that Choate knew from day to day where he stood.

When he was engrossed in an important or difficult case, he gave every minute of his time to it. In his later days he did almost no elementary law business, taking only cases which were already far along and in which he had been engaged by junior counsel. Often he was so overwhelmed with business that it was hard to hold him to his promise. But when he was really caught, his mind became a stream that took up a cause as if it were a ship, bearing it along night and day until some decision was reached. Every day he was thus absorbed anew in the affairs of some one else, like an actor in a succession of rôles, throwing himself each morning into a fresh part by a process of miraculous concentration.

After his interest had been aroused, the character of the tribunal made no difference to him. "The ablest argument I ever heard him make," said Chandler, "and perhaps the ablest it was ever my fortune to hear, was before a single judge at chambers, with no audience,— not even the presence of his own client. The amount involved was comparatively small; but the question interested his mind." Often he toiled feverishly on a case which seemed paltry, but it was always because he was attracted by some special or peculiar feature.

The layman,—and even the lawyer,—is sure to be astonished by the variety of cases in which Choate was employed. We live in an age of specialization, when a young graduate of Harvard Law School is likely to narrow his practice down to some limited field, such as that covering admiralty, or contracts, or real estate. Choate was versed in every phase of the profession. He was for the defendant in cases of divorce, embezzlement, assault, arson, and murder; he was ready to appear in any court, from that of a Justice of the Peace to that of a Supreme Court Judge; his clients represented an infinite variety of persons, from the lowest to the highest, from rogues to martyrs. He defended a Catholic priest against a charge of criminal assault; he conducted a case for Iasigi, a Greek, against a defendant who had induced the foreigner to sell goods on credit to an insolvent purchaser; and he represented one of the litigants in a quarrel between two branches of a great Christian Church. Studying the cases in which Rufus Choate appeared, we shall be ranging over nearly every aspect of human life, rich with material as interesting as that in the *Newgate Calendar*, or in a physician's notebook. Choate, at various times, was psychologist, sociologist, neurologist, alienist, and father confessor, as well as attorney.

Choate had a lofty conception of the dignity of

his profession, and I can find no instance of his being actuated by any but the most laudable motives. With him it was the victory which counted,—that, in itself, regardless of the fee involved, was worth the fight. Like any true artist, he was far more interested in his work than in any reward, tangible or intangible. Wendell Phillips, whose opinions on most subjects differed from those of Choate, once referred to the latter as the man "who made it safe to murder, and of whose health thieves asked before they began to steal." But it was not in Choate's nature to practice trickery or deception in order to set criminals free. He did believe that it was his duty, in the interests of justice, to do his best for a client accused of crime, and, like other famous and honorable lawyers, including the incomparable Erskine, he felt that even the guiltiest scoundrel was entitled to the benefit of the ablest possible counsel. But there came a moment in Choate's career when he was reluctant to undertake the defense of a person whom he did not consider innocent. While he still recognized the fairness of allowing an assassin the best of legal advice, he preferred to avoid such cases. He would not admit that he was bound to go into court and assert what he did not believe to be the truth.

It was this feeling, more than any other, which induced him to decline the defense of Professor Webster,

[141]

of Harvard, when the latter was on trial for the murder of Dr. Parkman. Both Franklin Dexter and Charles Sumner, convinced of Webster's innocence, urged Choate to take the case, and the former argued with him for three hours in an effort to persuade him. At the close of Dexter's presentation, Choate rose, walked two or three times up and down his library, and began, "Well, Brother Dexter, how do you answer these questions?" He then proceeded to advance query after query, showing some of the insuperable difficulties on the side of the defense. Dexter sat, depressed and silent, and finally, conceding the validity of Choate's logic, abandoned his errand. In the end, as everybody knows, Webster was convicted and executed.

We are hampered in our analysis of Choate's methods by the fact that most of his arguments were neither adequately reported nor written out by him; accordingly we are obliged to rely on the somewhat meager accounts which have come down to us from various unofficial sources. Some of the trials, however, have become historic in the annals of criminology and have been frequently reviewed. Of these perhaps the most startling is that of Albert J. Terrill, a wild young man of excellent family, charged, in 1845, with brutally slaying his mistress, Maria Bickford. The testimony seemed to be all against the prisoner. Although he had a wife and two small children in Weymouth, Massachusetts, Terrill, fascinated by Mrs. Bickford, had deserted his family in order to join her in a life of reckless debauchery. On a Sunday in October, he had visited her in a house of evil reputation occupied by Joel and Priscilla Lawrence, in Pinckney Lane, off Charles Street, in Boston; he was seen in her room at nine o'clock that evening; and then, between four and five on the next morning, old Joel was awakened by somebody stumbling down the stairs and a cry of "Fire!" from his wife. After he and a neighbor had extinguished three small blazes on the top floor, he entered Mrs. Bickford's room and was confronted by her body, slightly burned and blackened, with the throat cut from ear to ear by a razor. The wash-bowl contained bloody water, and there were matches in the straw mattress. Everything about the crime was peculiarly atrocious.

An immediate search for Terrill disclosed the fact that, about five o'clock that morning, he had hired a carriage of Fullam's Stable, in Bowdoin Square, volunteering the information that some one had broken into his room and tried to assault him. He then disappeared and could not be found, but, in his absence, he was formally indicted, and two months later he was arrested in New Orleans and brought back to Boston. When he came up for trial, with the distinguished

Samuel D. Parker as prosecuting attorney, it looked as if he could not escape the gallows. The evidence was, of course, all circumstantial, for there had been no witnesses of the act. Furthermore, in view of Terrill's passionate affection for Maria Bickford, there seemed to be no explicable motive for such a gory deed. Nevertheless there were few readers of newspapers in the state who did not believe Terrill to be guilty.

The prosecution, however, had reckoned without the genius of Rufus Choate. Retained for the defense by the wealthy Terrill family, Choate threw himself into the case, studying carefully all its possibilities. The crime itself was a vile one,—"murder and arson committed in a low brothel,"—yet, as Choate depicted it in the courtroom, it was transformed through his imagination into one of the great tragedies of the world, fit to stand beside those of Romeo and Juliet or of Tristram and Isolt. The worthless Terrill became an Othello, caught in the web of circumstance. By the mere vibrations of his melodious voice, Choate roused the emotions of pity and of terror, making his audience feel, when he said, "Albert *loved* Maria!" as if they were listening to some tale of helpless human victims pursued by Fate. Terrill, as Choate related the story, "was fascinated by the wiles of the unhappy female whose death was so awful; he loved her with the love

[144]

of forty thousand brothers, though alas, it was not as pure as it was passionate." And so, with the skill of a supreme artist, he gradually built up a picture of the events as he wished the jurymen to see them.

Choate's one hope of success was to convince the jury that there was ground of reasonable doubt as to Terrill's guilt, and it was this point that he reiterated again and again during the trial. It may, he hinted, have been a well-planned suicide. The crime may have been perpetrated by some third person for the purpose of robbery,—and here Choate suggested that the characters of Joel and Priscilla Lawrence were not above reproach. And then he struck a dramatic note by introducing evidence to prove that Terrill had been in the habit of walking in his sleep, and had actually, while in this state, attempted acts of violence. Was it not possible that Terrill, in a somnambulistic trance, had unwittingly committed the evil deed? To demonstrate what somnambulists have done, Choate read a splendidly vivid passage from Harvey's *Meditations* describing the attack of one sleeping hunter upon another. "This I mention," he went on, "as a proof that nothing hinders us, even from being assassins of others or murderers of ourselves, amid the mad follies of sleep, only the protecting care of our Heavenly Father!"

Choate paid very little attention to his client after

he had undertaken his defense. On the final morning, however, he stepped to the prisoner's dock and asked, "Well, sir, are you ready to make a strong push for life with me to-day?" Terrill not unnaturally replied in the affirmative. "Very well," answered Choate, "we will make it." . . . The argument which followed has been described by those who heard it as one of his most brilliant efforts. With consummate skill he reviewed the evidence, stressing the complete absence of a satisfactory motive, the failure of the prosecution to prove that Terrill was the murderer, and the possibility that the crime might have been committed by somebody else. In sonorous tones he emphasized the responsibility that rested upon the twelve men who were to decide Terrill's fate. "Every juror," he declared earnestly, "when he puts into the urn the verdict of 'Guilty,' writes upon it also, 'Let him die!'" And then, quietly but no less impressively, he closed, "Under the iron law of Rome, it was the custom to bestow a civic wreath upon him who should save the life of a citizen. Do your duty this day, gentlemen, and you too may deserve the civic crown."

The jury, after remaining out two hours, brought in a verdict of "Not Guilty," and, a few months later, when Terrill was again brought to trial on a charge of arson, Choate was once more his attorney and succeeded in having his client acquitted. For his accomplishment

[146]

in setting Terrill free, Choate was subjected to severe criticism; and indeed, from the layman's point of view, it did seem as if the law had been cheated, as if Rufus Choate, by his clever machinations, had subverted the ends of justice. But Choate's fellow lawyers, at that day and in our own time, have asserted that no other verdict was warranted by the testimony presented. The foreman of the jury was reported as having said that the issue of somnambulism was ignored by himself and his associates in reaching a decision. Choate himself was not the man to snatch from punishment a person of whose guilt he had no doubt. It was the hesitation in his own mind which enabled him to persuade the jury that the charge of murder was not definitely proved.

A case which has always attracted the attention of lawyers is that of William Wyman, President of the Phoenix Bank of Charlestown, who was indicted in 1843 for the embezzlement of funds of his institution. The counsel for the defense included Franklin Dexter, Daniel Webster, Ebenezer Rockwood Hoar, and Rufus Choate,—a formidable array of legal ability, with District Attorney Asahel R. Huntington conducting the prosecution. It was tried three times,—at Concord, at Lowell, and then again at Concord. On the first occasion, there occurred an interesting incident related by Senator George F. Hoar. Webster, in his concluding argument, had maintained that no trace of the money had been found in Wyman's possession. When Huntington had an opportunity to reply, he said vigorously, "They want to know what's become of the money. I can tell you what's become of the money. Five thousand dollars to one counsel, three thousand dollars to another, two thousand to another," waving his hand in succession towards Webster and Dexter and Choate. Although Choate only smiled and said nothing, and Dexter merely muttered, "This is beneath our notice," Webster was indignant and, rising to his feet, cried, "Am I to sit here to hear myself charged with sharing the spoils with a thief?" The presiding judge warned the District Attorney to confine himself to the evidence, but it took Webster a long time to forget his rage.

At this first trial, the jury disagreed, but, at the second, a new District Attorney, named Wells, conducted the prosecution and succeeded in getting a conviction, even against the gifted counsel for the defense. The case now came up again, on appeal, at Concord, with Choate bearing the chief burden for his side. In conducting his cross-examination of the bank directors,— witnesses for the Government,—Choate managed to make each one of them deny that he had consented to let Wyman have the right to dispose of the funds of the bank. Having done this, he showed that, as the funds, according to their own testimony, had never been under Wyman's control or in his possession, he could not be convicted of embezzlement. The court so held and directed an acquittal. Choate's shrewd management of his case aroused the admiration of his fellow members of the Boston Bar.

Webster and Choate were not always on the same side. During the hot summer of 1847, the two men were pitted against each other in the Oliver Smith Will Case, tried before the Supreme Judicial Court, at Northampton. A bachelor, Oliver Smith, with many poor relatives who had hoped for legacies from him, died at the age of eighty, leaving his fortune of nearly $400,000 to various local charities. The heirs at law attempted to break the will, and employed Rufus Choate as Senior Counsel. The odds were undeniably against him, not merely because he was opposed by Daniel Webster, but also because his case was none too strong. Choate contended that the will was invalid because one of the three witnesses was not, at the moment of attestation, of sound mind. The witness in question was Theophilus Parsons Phelps, grandson of the hypochondriacal Chief Justice Theophilus Parsons, of the Massachusetts Bench. A year before the document was drawn, Phelps had been regarded by the Superintendent of the State Asylum as insane, but the evidence of his recovery was good.

[149]

Choate, nevertheless, delivered an impassioned speech of three hours or more, in which he made a psychical study of Phelps's malady. The jury and the audience were obviously much impressed by what Choate had said, and he would have won the case had not Webster resorted to the audacious expedient of bringing Phelps himself to the witness stand. It is characteristic of Choate that he promised Webster not to interrogate the young man in any way that would injure his feelings. Phelps, undisturbed by Choate, told his story with composure. Then Judge Wilde, reviewing the evidence in a dry and unemotional manner, brought the jury back from Choate's rhetoric to the facts at issue. As a result, the verdict was given for the defendants, and Choate, in part because of his generous attitude towards the essential witness, lost the case.

During this dramatic trial, Webster, who had himself a gift for fervent declamation, made no attempt to rival Choate in oratory, but contented himself with a simple statement of the situation as he saw it. As a matter of fact, it was the only sensible way of opposing Choate. When Choate had concluded his flights of eloquence, Webster congratulated his learned brother on his imaginative power and poetical fancy, and then went on,—"And now, gentlemen, we are called upon to consider a question, not of poetry, but of fact. This is a simple matter, which concerns plain people,—like you and me. Let's get down to real business." It was Webster's plan thus to unweave or tear away the magic veil with which Choate had surrounded the ordinary details of the case. When Choate had elevated the affair into the sphere of romance, Webster would drag it back ruthlessly to the low level of common life, like a necromancer speaking a charm of disenchantment. But he always respected and feared Choate's resourcefulness. Once, while listening to one of Choate's florid harangues, he turned to the junior counsel by his side and said, "Some of our technical brethren would call that all flimsy humbug; if it be so, which I deny, it is still humbug which stirs men's souls to their inmost depths. It is reason impelled by passion, by legal learning, and adorned by fancy." On another occasion, Webster, conversing with Peter Harvey, said, "It is a great mistake to suppose that Mr. Choate, in that flowery elocution, does not keep his logic all right. Amid all that pile of flowers there is a strong, firm chain of logic."

Nor was Choate, with all his reverence for Webster, to be put down or overwhelmed by his greatness. The story is told of a famous trial during which Choate had presented the law with a lucidity and an emphasis which were impressive. Webster, the opposing counsel, turned on him the gaze of his mournful eyes, as if in mute remonstrance against such a gross perversion. Noticing the glance, Choate advanced a step and, looking directly at Webster, thundered, "That *is* the law, may it please your Honor, in spite of the admonishing, the somewhat *paternal* look in the eye of my illustrious friend."

Another interesting dispute over a will was the Phillips Case, argued by Choate at Ipswich during the summer of 1849. The testator, a Mr. Phillips, of Nahant, had committed suicide, leaving a fortune of nearly a million dollars, some of it to his immediate family but the bulk to a wealthy relative. The heirs at law tried to break the will on the ground that the deceased Phillips was insane, that he had been unduly influenced, and,—strange anticlimax,—that the document was void because it was signed on a Sunday. The argument for the plaintiffs was presented by W. H. Gardner, in a powerful appeal. Choate, representing the executors, then replied for the defense, in another of those speeches which were not preserved for posterity but which, in the estimate of those who heard them, were scintillating with sparkling phrases. In trenchant language he ridiculed the contention that a paper executed on Sunday must therefore be illegal. The jury gave him a verdict within a very few minutes.

In the spring of 1851, Choate appeared in defense

of his own pastor, the Reverend Dr. Adams, in a suit for slander brought against him by a man named Fairchild. Fairchild, a clergyman of South Boston, had been accused by a certain Rhoda Davidson of being the father of her illegitimate son. He paid her part of the large sum which she demanded and wrote her a letter which seemed to be a confession. Later, when the facts were made public, he tried to commit suicide, but failed, and was expelled from the ministry by an ecclesiastical council. Indicted in Boston for adultery, he remained for some time outside of Massachusetts, but eventually returned and was acquitted, chiefly because the testimony of the most important witness, Rhoda Davidson, was impeached. He then received a call to return to his pulpit in South Boston, and a council duly called advised that he should be settled in his parish, taking the position that his exoneration in the courts should be regarded as proof of his innocence. With this conclusion, Dr. Adams did not agree. Fairchild, after he had been installed again in South Boston, requested the Suffolk South Association, which had also expelled him, to rescind their vote. At a hearing which followed, Dr. Adams presented his reasons for opposing Fairchild's reinstatement; whereupon Fairchild singled Adams out as a man of influence and sued him for slander.

[153]

The case was heard before referees agreed upon by both parties concerned. Choate argued that the acquittal of a person charged with crime in a civil court ought not, *ipso facto*, to restore the defendant as a member of an ecclesiastical body, inasmuch as the rules of evidence and the causes for action are different in civil and ecclesiastical tribunals; and that an association of ministers has the privilege of inquiring into the conduct of its members and, if necessary, of passing a vote of expulsion. The referees decided that ministerial associations are not responsible to legal tribunals for the accuracy of their conclusions and accordingly made an award in favor of Dr. Adams,—a decision later sustained by the Court. In preparing his case, Choate was obliged to carry on an immense amount of research into the nature and history of associations of ministers and their relation to the churches with which they were connected.

The modern city lawyer of established reputation is not likely to accept many slander suits, but he is even less likely to appear for the defense in a charge of criminal assault. This, however, Rufus Choate did. Father John B. Gillespie, a Roman Catholic priest, walking along a side street in Boston on a moonlit night on his way to administer the last rites to a dying member of his parish and absorbed in meditation, accidentally brushed against a Mrs. Towle, who was strolling with her husband. The woman misconstrued the push, and the husband insulted Father Gillespie, who, stung by the undeserved attack, applied an uncomplimentary epithet to Mrs. Towle. Towle then called out, "Stop the rascal, he has insulted my wife!"; whereupon three young men, described by Choate as having "feet like those of elephants and fists like the paws of lions," rushed up and kicked and beat the priest until he ran for his life, only to be seized by a passing night watchman, incarcerated, and brought up on the following morning before the Police Court, where, to quote Choate once more, "ten thousand arrows of ten thousand libels were instantly launched at him." The case was tried before a jury composed of Protestants, the foreman being an orthodox deacon, at a time when denominational prejudice was supposed to be violent; and Choate's task had its problems. His summing up for the defense was, when all the conditions are considered, a model of persuasive eloquence. He dwelt at length on the previous good reputation of Father Gillespie, on the total absence of any adequate incentive to such an assault, and on the existence of controlling restraints against any such action. With graceful tact, he said, "I have proved to you, gentlemen, that this collision was purely an accident; such an accident, Mr. Foreman, as might have

[155]

happened to you or to me returning from a Union meeting, or a Liberty meeting, or a Jenny Lind concert, or what is infinitely better, *a monthly concert of prayer,*"—advancing, as he repeated the last phrase, nearer to the deacon, as if to win from him the sympathy of one who was familiar with the absorption with divine things which usually follows the monthly concert of prayer in all Congregational churches. Noticing the obvious hostility in the expression of another juror, Choate walked directly up to him and shouted, "Sir, I have the utmost confidence that I can satisfy you on this, as well as on every other point of the case; lend me your ear." He closed with a subtle plea to the jury not to be affected by any feeling of religious bigotry, but to form an opinion solely as to whether the public peace had been violated. The jury disagreed, and the matter was never again brought up for trial,—thus virtually giving the victory to Choate.

Perhaps the case of Choate's which aroused the most widespread public interest was the divorce suit brought by Frank Dalton against his wife, Helen Gove Dalton, in 1857, Choate appearing for the defense. Nearly two years before, Dalton, having uncovered what he thought to be a guilty intrigue between his wife and a youth named Sumner, had induced his brother-in-law, Coburn, to join him in luring Sumner to Coburn's house,

[156]

where the two men attacked him and beat him severely, —so severely that he was later taken ill and died. Dalton, arrested and tried for manslaughter, was acquitted, but he did plead guilty to a charge of assault and battery and was condemned to imprisonment for five months. It was soon after, and while he was still in jail, that Dalton sought a divorce. The counsel for the plaintiff was Richard Henry Dana, Jr., the author of *Two Years Before the Mast* and a lawyer of high standing at the Boston Bar. The newspapers, with less efficiency but with the same morbidity and sensationalism shown by the tabloids in our time, furnished their greedy readers with all the salacious morsels which they could find. Large sums were offered merely for standing room in the Boston Court House, and, once in, no man could get out without becoming a shadow.

In the courtroom throughout the proceedings was Mrs. Dalton, a young and charming woman, accompanied and guarded by her mother and her sister, Mrs. Coburn. In his summing-up,—which lasted two full days,—Choate emphasized and reiterated two points: first, that Helen Dalton, although indiscreet, foolish, and susceptible to flattery, was, in her intimacy with Sumner, not guilty of adultery; second, that Dalton himself had conceded her innocence by taking her back to live with him for a period of several weeks and had

[157]

written her, from his cell, letters indicating the deepest affection,—letters "so beautiful, so manly, one long, unbroken strain of sweet music, the burthen of which is home, sweet home." In planting these two ideas in the minds of the jurymen, Choate employed every known advocate's device: he crumbled the evidence of two witnesses who claimed to have heard Mrs. Dalton's confession; he dragged Coburn into court and compelled him to admit that he had lied to Mrs. Dalton's father in order to extort from him money and clothing; he used sarcasm and raillery and pathos and denunciation, keeping his audience always entertained and running the gamut from laughter to tears. . . . As the shadows of the second evening fell he concluded with a solemnity which hushed the courtroom:

For no levity, no vanity, no indiscretion, let there be a divorce. I bring to your minds the words of Him who spake as never man spake: "Whosoever putteth away his wife"—for vanity, for coquetry, for levity, for flirtation—whosoever putteth away his wife for anything short of adultery, and that established by clear, undoubted, and credible proof,—whosoever does it, "causeth her to commit adultery." If they may not be dismissed then, gentlemen, to live again together, for her sake and her parents' sake, sustain her. Give her back to self-respect, and the assistance of that public opinion which all of us require.

The Dalton Case, although exceptional in some respects, had little about it to distinguish it from a thousand other similar divorce actions. It was the personality and vitality of Rufus Choate which stirred up excitement and filled the pages of the Boston newspapers. It was said that he defended Mrs. Dalton as if she had been his daughter or his sister. The advocate was, for once, greater than his cause, and gave it an importance which it would otherwise have lacked. He did not argue in vain, for the jury disagreed, and the divorce was not granted. It has been stated that the Daltons were later reunited and lived happily ever after. Let us hope so for the sake of the climax which that story affords.

While Rufus Choate was doubtless at his best in an argument before a jury, he appeared in many important cases before the higher courts of Massachusetts and of the United States. Early in 1846, for example, he was associated with Webster in arguing the famous case of *Rhode Island* v. *Massachusetts*, the former state having brought a bill in equity complaining that an error had been made in the original boundary line between the two states and asking for a restoration of the disputed territory. Involving, as it did, a dispute between sovereign states, the decision was of high significance, and the matter had been pending for twenty years. Be-

fore Choate was employed in it, the Supreme Court had
decided that it had jurisdiction in cases involving boundary lines between states,—this in spite of Webster's
able argument to the contrary. The hearing was to have
been held in February, 1844, but it was postponed after
Choate had spent a month in preparation and had withdrawn temporarily from the Senate Chamber in order
to get his brief in order. It was finally held in February,
1846, with Richard K. Randolph and John Whipple
representing Rhode Island. Although no fragment of
Choate's argument has ever been found among his manuscripts, we know that he made a real impression on the
court, especially on Judge Catron, who declared afterwards, "I have heard the most eminent advocates, but
he surpasses them all." The New York *Express*, in its
account of the case, said that Choate's plea was "adorned
with all that was able in logic and beautiful in imagery."
Alexander H. Stephens, an excellent critic, listened to
him with delight and said, "From the moment he commenced, he enchained the audience and enlivened the
dull subject by apt historical allusions and pleasing illustrations. . . . Every paragraph was as the turning of
a kaleidoscope, where new and brilliant images are presented at every turn." The bill was ultimately dismissed by Justice Taney on the ground that "this court,
under the Constitution of the United States, have not

the power to try such a question between States, or redress such a wrong, even if the wrong is proved to have been done."

In the noteworthy case of *Thurlow* v. *Massachusetts*, heard first in 1845, Choate and Webster, as joint counsel, argued against the validity of Massachusetts statutes which virtually nullified certain liquor laws passed by Congress. The plaintiff had been indicted and convicted for selling spirits without the license required by the state for dispensing any quantity less than twenty-eight gallons. Some of the sales charged in the indictment were of foreign liquors; and this introduced the question as to whether the state law was repugnant to Acts of Congress authorizing the importation of wines, brandies, and other foreign spirits. Massachusetts, represented by the able John Davis, was urging upon the Supreme Court the strictest possible interpretation of the Constitution,—indeed taking what amounted to an extreme States Rights position. Choate, on the contrary, maintained that any Congressional act permitting the importation of goods on the payment of duties automatically allowed the importer to sell those goods, and that any state statute interrupting the chain of traffic from the importer to the ultimate consumer was unconstitutional. His speech on the question, according to a correspondent, was "very able, ingenious,

[161]

and beautiful." Unfortunately the Court, because of two vacancies on the Bench, ordered a reargument, which came in 1847, when Choate was not available. Eventually the state statutes were upheld, and the power of individual states over retail trade in spirits was settled, —that is, until the passage of the 18th Amendment. The opinions of the judges in this case cover sixty-six pages in the *Decisions of the Supreme Court of the United States*.

Another issue of much importance developed in the case of *Norris* v. *Boston*, in connection with certain immigrant laws passed by Massachusetts, especially the so-called Passenger Law of 1837, laying a tax of two dollars on each immigrant. The problem had many of the same features presented by the South Carolina statutes excluding free negroes from entry into that state,— statutes which had been declared unconstitutional by Judge Johnson, in 1823, in the United States Circuit Court. Norris had brought suit against the City of Boston to recover $38 paid by him under the act. He had won in the Court of Common Pleas, and the decision was reaffirmed by the Supreme Judicial Court of Massachusetts, on the ground that the Passenger Law was unconstitutional. On an appeal, it was argued before the Supreme Court of the United States in February, 1847, with Webster and Choate for the plaintiff against John Davis. After some reargument, in which the burden rested on Webster, a decision, rendered in 1849, declared, by a vote of five to four, that the Massachusetts law was unconstitutional. It was felt at the time that this decision, sweeping away, as it did, all laws for the exclusion of colored persons from any state, was to be far-reaching in the effects, and it was severely criticized in the South. Choate agreed with Webster that it was incomprehensible how any Massachusetts General Court could have passed the original Passenger Law.

Of no less historical interest was the remarkable Methodist Church Case, resulting from a breach between the Northern and Southern branches of that organization over a matter of slavery. A General Conference held in 1844 had outlined a plan for a division and had provided for the distribution of property, especially that of the Book Concern, which carried on publishing under church auspices. The Southern agents of the Methodist Church brought suit against this Book Concern for the delivery of their share of the property, the separation of the two branches having been ratified by General Conferences both in the North and in the South. Choate, appearing in 1851 for the defendants, —the Northern side,—told his clients that it was the greatest case he had ever studied, and spent even more

[163]

time than usual in preparation. During the trial, he was taken ill and obliged to retire to his New York hotel. When the physician came, he prescribed calomel, and asked, "How large a dose have you been accustomed to?" "I don't know," answered Choate, "but give me the largest dose you ever gave a man in your life!"

Because of his indisposition, the Court adjourned from Friday to Monday, and Choate, although looking worn and weary, was able to present himself at the appointed hour; and, in spite of his illness, he argued for two whole days, growing stronger as he proceeded. In his opening remarks, he spoke regretfully of the events "of sad and singular interest" which had led to the dismemberment of the great Methodist Church. Then, turning to technical matters, he maintained that the resolutions of the General Conference of 1844 gave an assent to the division only on certain conditions, most of which had not been met, and that this Conference, under the circumstances, had no authority to allow the separation. His conclusion, after an elaborate array of precedents, was that the separation of the South was an unauthorized withdrawal,—a secession,—and that the Book Concern need not make the transfer of property demanded. The logic was apparent on his side, but the decision of Justice Nelson,—and later of the Supreme Court of the United States,—was against Choate.

When he was about to leave New York on the day following the trial, his clients handed him $2,000, telling him never to abandon the case while there was a higher tribunal to which it could be appealed. "I declare," commented Choate, "these religious people fight harder and pay better than any clients I ever knew."

A mere cursory mention of the interesting cases in which Rufus Choate was a protagonist would require volumes instead of a single chapter. Sometimes a minor litigation, even more than a great issue, would display his peculiar powers. In the Crafts Case, it was alleged that the owner of a vessel had conspired with her captain to cast her away on the reefs of Cape Cod in order to collect her insurance. Robert Rantoul, Jr., United States District Attorney, conducted the prosecution, his chief witness being a man named Wilson, who had turned State's Evidence. Choate's chief hope was to discredit Wilson's testimony. This he did, first of all, by a grueling cross-examination, which revealed Wilson's very shady past, and secondly, by a closing argument in which he branded Wilson as a vagabond and a villain, who had interwoven truth with "the scarlet tissue of falsehood." When Choate wished to appear in the guise of a denunciator, he could be as terrible as the Recording Angel, and his tongue had the edge of a Damascus blade. "This Wilson," he cried, "is wholly uncorroborated and discredited. They brought him to curse, and behold he hath blessed us altogether!" It is small wonder that the jury, their minds filled with the infamy of Wilson, declared that Crafts was innocent.

There was a period, especially after 1850, when Choate was retained in several important patent cases, and might almost have been said to have made that branch of the law his specialty. In *Woodbury* v. *Allen*, he was for the plaintiff, who owned a patent which he was trying to protect. Against the opposing counsel, who had warned the jury about the oration which Choate was sure to make, the latter was exceedingly clever. Disavowing all intention of being eloquent, he introduced in the course of his disclaimer a splendid and moving disquisition upon inventors and the dependence of the country upon them and their works. In March, 1852, at Trenton, New Jersey, he appeared in the great india-rubber case of *Goodyear* v. *Day*, he being for the defendant, with Webster,—whose last courtroom appearance it was destined to be,—for the plaintiff. Webster, who was then Secretary of State, had been offered a fee of $10,000, with $5,000 additional if he secured a verdict for Goodyear,—and he won his case and the extra money in spite of all that Rufus Choate could do.

Perhaps the last really memorable case in which Choate was engaged was that of *Shaw* v. *Worcester Rail-*

Rufus Choate in His Prime as an Orator, from a Photograph

road, argued in the spring of 1858, in which Mrs. Shaw was suing for damages for the death of her husband, who had been killed at a railroad crossing. Choate, representing the plaintiff, described the accident in characteristic language:

On came the terrible glare of the engine,—that fire of hell! There was no curving board of warning to him who would cross that track. There was no proud arch to bid him stay,—no friendly flag-man. Then blew no whistle—that would have startled all but the dead; then comes the collision—the wagon and the engine; and it is not the giant that dies, but the weak!

In the course of the trial, one witness testified that Shaw was intoxicated while he was driving, adding that he had smelled gin and brandy on the victim's breath after the accident. This gave Choate an opportunity for the display of his resourcefulness. "This witness," he cried, "swears that he stood by the dying man in his last moments. What was he there for? Was it to administer those assiduities which are ordinarily proffered at the bedside of dying men? Was it to extend to him the consolations of that religion which for eighteen hundred years has comforted the world? No, gentlemen, no! He leans over the departing sufferer; he bends his face nearer and nearer to him,—and what

[167]

does he do? What does he do, I ask?—Smells gin and brandy!" This was a ridiculous anticlimax, the effect of which was to make the jury forget the real evidence. Choate won his case, but it was appealed and tried several times more, the jury giving each time higher damages, until the defendant was finally obliged to pay the sum of $20,000.

During those crowded years from 1846 to 1859, Rufus Choate was an exceedingly busy man with his professional responsibilities alone, to say nothing of the other insistent demands upon his time. He had very little leisure,—too little ever to get really rested. A letter to his son, Rufus, written September 24, 1854, describes his usual mood:

I have just finished an insurance trial of some ten or eleven days, very *scraggly* and ticklish—though a just claim—and won it, against a very strong charge of the judge. Then came another insurance case, when J. and I were for the office def't,—and had the good luck to get that too, in three or four hours. I had to snatch any moment to write a little address for Danvers. Altogether, therefore, I am utterly prostrated and unstrung. I would give a thousand dollars, if I could afford it, for an undisturbed rest of a week.

He wrote, in a fragment of an essay, that the vacations of a lawyer are "divers infinitely minute particles

of time,—half-hours before breakfast, or after dinner,
Saturdays at evening, intervals between the going out
of one client and the coming in of another"; and he told
Judge Warren that he was hoping to write a book on
the subject "The Lawyer's Vacation," in which he
planned to show that the lawyer's only respite is the space
between the question put to a witness and his answer!
. . . But somehow he could always get refreshment
from literature. It was in the very lecture at Danvers
mentioned in the letter above that he described his own
experience:

Let the case of a busy lawyer testify to the priceless value
of the love of reading. He comes home, his temples throb-
bing, his nerves shattered, from the trial of a week; surprised
and alarmed by the charge of the judge, and pale with anxiety
about the verdict of the next morning, not at all satisfied with
what he has done himself, though he does not yet see how he
could have improved it; recalling with dread and self-dis-
paragement, if not with envy, the brilliant effort of his antago-
nist, and tormenting himself with the vain wish that he could
have replied to it. . . . With a superhuman effort he opens
his book, and in the twinkling of an eye he is looking into the
full "orb of Homeric or Miltonic song," or he stands in the
crowd,—breathless, yet swayed as forests or the sea by winds,
—hearing and to judge the Pleadings for the Crown. . . .
and the courthouse is as completely forgotten as the dream of
a pre-adamite life. Well may he prize that endeared charm,

[169]

so effectual and safe, without which the brain had long ago been chilled by paralysis, or set on fire of insanity!

It is impossible to reckon the number of cases in which Choate appeared during this very active period, for he kept no record of them himself, and many of them were never reported. Neilson states that there are 333 causes in which he was counsel and argued questions of law and equity which had been printed in the State and Federal *Reports*. But this takes no account of his jury trials. He was busy, of course,—and yet, if he had been questioned, he would not have had it otherwise. Like most men who are grumbling about overwork, he could not have endured idleness. He had to go on, for labor was his greatest pleasure. He had to take new cases, or he would have sunk into decay. He was the most restless of men, never happy unless he was occupied; and he seized hopefully upon each new case as if it were, in a sense, a vacation from the one before it. He would have sympathized with Tennyson's Ulysses, when he cried:

> How dull it is to pause, to make an end,
> To rust unburnished, not to shine in use
> As though to breathe were life.

We need have no pity for Rufus Choate!

CHAPTER VIII

Persuading a Jury

H OW are we, three-quarters of a century later, to recapture the magnetism, the flame and fury, which distinguished Rufus Choate in his prime? No phonograph has preserved the tones of that mellifluous voice; there is no motion picture to display him to us in action. But we do know, from those who heard and saw him, that he was the most persuasive of speakers, with a power over an indifferent or hostile jury which has been compared to the fascination of a bird by a snake. This was what he loved. "No gambler," wrote Senator Hoar, "ever hankered for the feverish delight of the gaming table as Choate did for that absorbing game, half chance, half skill, where twelve human dice must all turn up together one way, or there is no victory." Something of an actor he must have been, and most of what he did,—his smiles, his asides, his apparently careless gestures,—was done consciously, for the effect which it would produce on the jury. Stone said of him, "Choate's extravagance was always design. His eye

[171]

and mind, in their wildest flights, were on the jury. He was in pursuit of their verdict. He meant to have it, and he generally got it." As if by some occult instinct, he could tell when a juryman was against him, and he frequently turned to such an obstinate fellow openly, singling him out for conversion.

Again and again he triumphed under conditions completely adverse. It was usually his plan to win the jury at the outset. "If you haven't got hold of them, got their convictions at least open, in your first half hour or hour," he said frequently, "you will never get them at all." . . . And yet there was an exceptional situation, when this method did not succeed. Whipple, who understood all his idiosyncrasies, remembered a battle of wills between Choate and a jury foreman, a hard-headed, defiant business man, who could not comprehend a mind differing so essentially from his own. Choate's argument, so far as facts were concerned, was done in an hour; yet he continued, aware that the foreman was unconvinced and determined to break down his resistance. For five hours he talked, gliding his way subtly into the man's confidence, until at last the face of the obstructive juror indicated agreement with the advocate's views. By sheer persistence, Rufus Choate had won!

With masterly strategy, Choate never showed his

[172]

full hand. His was the art which conceals art. Again and again a juryman would enter the box resolved to resist the great seducer. But Choate carefully avoided giving the jury the impression that he was about to attack them. He would begin in a conversational tone as if he were about to take them into his confidence, complimenting them on their courtesy and intelligence, appealing craftily to their pride, and addressing them from time to time directly, with such remarks as, "Now, Mr. Foreman, what do you think of that proposition?" or, "You see, gentlemen, just how it was," or, "Be patient with me just a little longer, if you can." It was as if he were acting towards them in a fraternal way, as one equal would treat another. Having gripped their attention, he would slip unobtrusively into the argument, and, almost without realizing it, the juror who had hardened his heart against Choate's wiles would soften until he yielded fully and gladly to the enchantment of the magician. Once, after such an obstinate juryman had joined in giving a verdict for Choate's client, somebody expressed wonder that he could so readily agree with his associates. "Why," he replied naïvely, "the case was a plain one. Choate happened to be right this time. Let him come before me in a case where he is palpably wrong, like the Terrill trial, and I'll resist him. He never can humbug me!"

[173]

It was indeed a high degree of art which could thus remove a victim's prejudices without allowing him to know that the operation had been performed.

As he went along, he dominated the situation, turning from judge to jury and from jury to audience, noticing the slightest evidence of favorable or adverse emotion as revealed in their faces. Like an experienced general, he had always a theory around which all his tactics must be centered, and he would not allow himself, except for good reason, to be diverted into side paths. When all the testimony was available on both sides, he would build it into the structure which he wished to create, emphasizing this and eliminating that, often not disclosing fully to his hearers what he was aiming to do, but invariably developing in the end a conception of the case which could be easily understood even by an obtuse mind. Choate had an uncanny perception of the motives and mental processes of the normal man, and his familiar colloquialisms never passed over the heads of the jury. Careful not to annoy or bully or patronize them, he kept to their level,—and they appreciated it. It is no wonder that it was said that he could almost have made a jury believe that the Siamese twins did not look alike and possibly that they never could have been born of the same mother.

Much of Choate's success must be attributed to the

thoroughness and intensity with which he prepared himself for the courtroom ordeal. Far from relying on the inspiration of the moment or trusting to his native fluency of utterance, he made a careful preliminary brief, and took during the trial the most copious notes which he spent each evening in collating and digesting. In court, as the evidence was being presented, he was scribbling sheet after sheet of paper in his illegible scrawl until, when the moment came for his summing-up, he had a pile of manuscript on the desk before him. While he was occupied with a case, he was completely absorbed in what was going on in connection with it, concentrating every fiber of his personality on the focal question. Once the trial had begun, and the jury was empaneled, nothing else could engage Choate's attention. "From that moment," said one of his students, "the client's interest was Choate's religion!"

Towards the presiding judge, no matter what his age or his reputation might be, Choate was uniformly deferential, even when his argument was interrupted; but there were occasions when he indulged in grimly humorous asides. His relations with Chief Justice Shaw, one of the gruffest of presiding judges, were notoriously amusing. Once, in his sly way, Choate said, "I always approach Judge Shaw as a savage approaches his fetish,—knowing that he is ugly, but feeling that he is great." His respect for the judge's high office was unbounded, and he would not allow himself to show anger in his presence. Once outside the courtroom, however, he would sometimes break out, "That judge is an old woman,—he's a fool,—he can't put two ideas together,—he isn't fair,—he's bigoted as the devil!" Again, when he had been severely rebuked by Chief Justice Shaw, Choate, who had listened patiently, turned to his associates near him and said in a low tone, "I do not suppose that any one ever thought the Chief Justice was much of a lawyer, but nobody can deny that he is a man of pleasant manners." But in his heart Choate had a lofty ideal of the judiciary, and his confidence in their decision was rarely shattered. When, in a famous trial, one of his junior counsel was rising to contest what seemed to him to be an unfair ruling by Justice Shaw, Choate drew him back saying, "Let it go. Sit down. Life, liberty, and property are always safe in his hands." One other story will perhaps illustrate his manner with judges. During the Crafts trial, Choate pressed the Court to make what he considered to be a very just order in regard to taking a deposition. The judge, in reply, suggested that the matter be postponed until the following day so that Choate might be able to bring in a precedent for such an action. "I will look, your Honor," answered Choate, "and endeavor to find a precedent if you require it; though it would seem a pity that the Court should lose the distinction of being the first to establish so just a rule."

Towards opposing counsel, Rufus Choate, even at the height of his fame, was benignly courteous unless provoked, in which case he could be stinging in his retaliation. Any attempted witticism at his expense was met by prompt and clever retort, and the danger of rousing him was well recognized by members of the Massachusetts Bar. Often, when his opponent was younger and less experienced than he, Choate could be almost fatherly in his manner, and no one was quicker to assist and encourage new competitors. Towards his equals, Choate was appreciative and polite, but he feared no one of them, not even Jeremiah Mason or Daniel Webster. He was seldom impatient, but he resented interruption, and, if he were stopped, he would place the blame on his opponent, saying, "I do not object to these interruptions except for the time they take," or, "These repeated interruptions only afford me a new opportunity to present my impregnable case. It will tire you, gentlemen of the jury; but my brother's interposition renders it necessary."

Occasionally an attorney would appear who seemed to know exactly how to annoy Choate and who, when the great advocate was getting under full steam towards

[177]

one of his magnificent climaxes, would ruthlessly inter-
rupt this flow of language in a cold manner and state
his objection, while the perspiring orator was held suspended, as it were, in mid-flight. When Choate was
thus challenged for the third time by some such adversary, he came to a dead stop and said, "Very well,—
if my brother proposes to argue for his client a little
more, I will sit down and wait," and he began to put on
one after one several of the coats which he had taken
off before going into action, making as much commo-
tion as possible and looking like a peevish child who
wished to place all the blame on somebody else. After
his rival had finished, Choate stood up, solemnly di-
vested himself of his layers of clothing, and said in a
grieved tone, "Oh, is that all? Why, what a trifle!
I'll give that point up, and let my brother have it just
as he's a mind to!" During these proceedings, while
Choate was emerging from one coat after another, the
court and jury were convulsed with laughter. . . .
And Choate had his sweet revenge. Not long after-
ward, when the other lawyer was strutting in a pompous
manner across Boston Common, some one, pointing him
out to Choate, said, "What do you imagine our friend
there is thinking about?" "Well," replied Choate
dryly, "I should guess, from his bearing, that he is wondering whether God made him or he made God!"

[178]

When Choate was really aroused, he had the ferocity of a tiger. In an important patent case, while he was making a brilliant, if somewhat rhetorical, argument, his opponent, sitting a little distance behind him, kept up a low derisive chuckle, and, when Choate was worked up to his highest fury, laughed audibly in a sneering way. Hardly pausing in his eloquence, Choate swung around, turned upon the discourteous attorney, and, advancing towards him a step or two while the audience sat in breathless silence, said in measured and dramatic tones, "Sir, let him laugh who wins!" The effect was prodigious. The man seemed to shrivel up beneath Choate's fiery eyes. The jury were brought to Choate's side,—and he received their verdict.

Instances of Choate's resourcefulness are repeated almost daily at the clubs where lawyers lunch in Boston. Pitted against an opponent whose voice was like the bellowing of a bull, he referred playfully to his adversary's "stentorian powers." The indignant orator arose and objected to Choate's comment, stating that nothing in his manner could have justified such a phrase. As his protests continued, he roared louder and louder, until the courthouse rang; and, when he was at his noisiest, Choate half rose, secured the judge's attention, and said, "One word, may it please the Court,—just one brief word, if my brother will allow. I see my mistake. I

[179]

beg leave to withdraw what I said." Under the circumstances, the effect was irresistible, and even the embarrassed speaker joined in the outburst of laughter.

It is frequently possible, as every trial lawyer knows, to injure an opposing witness's testimony even when its truth cannot be refuted. Of this art Choate was a supreme master. In the Terrill case, for instance, when all the evidence had apparently been introduced, the prosecuting attorney brought forward a resident of Roxbury to give evidence against Terrill. Now Roxbury, to-day a part of the city of Boston, was then only four miles from State Street. This fact was Choate's cue. "Where," he asked, "was this tardy and belated witness, that he comes here to tell us all he knows, and all he doesn't know, ·forty-eight hours after the evidence for the defense is closed? Is the case so obscure that he never heard of it? Was he ill or in custody? Was he in Europe, Asia, or Africa? Was he on the Red Sea, or the Yellow Sea, or the Black Sea, or the Mediterranean Sea?. . . . No, gentlemen, he was at none of these places (comparatively easy to access), but,—and I would call your attention, Mr. Foreman, to the fact, and urge it upon your attention,—he was at that remote, more inaccessible region, whence so few travelers return,—*Roxbury!*" If this seems to us like humor of the music hall variety, remember the place and the occasion,—and remember also that no juryman, hearing the witness's evidence, could help smiling inwardly, if not outwardly, as he thought of the long trip from Roxbury to Boston.

A similar situation arose in an insurance trial, when he had to deal with a witness who swore positively to the detriment of Choate's client, but who was obliged, on examination, to admit that his own character was not unspotted. Choate's only chance was to convince the jury that this rascally witness was perjuring himself. In his summary, he depicted vividly the vices and misdemeanors of which the man had confessed himself to be guilty, and then went on impressively, "Do you suppose, gentlemen, that in this vast violation of all the sentiments and virtues that bind men together in civil society, *veracity* alone would survive the chaos of *such* a character?—'the last rose of summer' on *such* a soil?" The jury caught his point, and were dubious about the truth of the testimony,—and once more Choate won his case!

There were periods, after his first appearance in Boston, when his novel methods of speaking excited prejudice against him, and when rival attorneys were amused by him to the point of risibility. He had certain mannerisms which were unusual. In one address at

Worcester it was said that he split his coat in two in the back, from collar to waistband. Sometimes, if he felt his energy flagging, he would give two or three convulsive jerks of his whole body, as if every bone were being shaken from its socket, and then start again, apparently renewed by this stimulating spasm; he would bow to the floor and straighten himself up again, as if he were a jackknife opening and closing; and then, as he finished an intense outburst, he would rise on his heels and, throwing his head back like some highbred racer, would draw in his breath through his nostrils with a noise which could be heard all over the room. In moments of strong emotion, his extended arm would tremble and vibrate, as if in accord with the storm in his soul. At times every muscle would seem to be brought into play, and the perspiration would fall in drops from his hair and down his face. Again he would rise on his toes and close a sentence by coming down on his heels with a force which frightened the timid. Wendell Phillips once compared him to a monkey with convulsions. . . . But it was not long before even his opponents forgot his idiosyncrasies and saw only his shining eyes. "Why do you endure such treatment?" asked a friend, after Choate had been the victim of impertinence from a lawyer long established at the Bar. "Why do you not retort?" "I shall retort by winning the case," was

[182]

Choate's reply. It was the kind of answer which his critics were likely to understand.

The very extravagance of his manner occasionally made Choate vulnerable. Once, after Choate had been especially florid and impassioned, his opponent, the wily Jeremiah Mason, rose, and with his homely nasal twang, said, "And now, gentlemen of the jury, I don't know as I can *gyrate* afore you as my friend Choate does; but I want to state *jest a few simple pints.*" The effect was like the puncturing of a large toy balloon. In a similar situation, when Choate had let loose a flood of rhetoric in an important case, his opponent declared that "it was altogether too great a boo for so small a calf!" It cannot be said, however, that there were many lawyers who got the better of Rufus Choate.

In the gentle art of examining witnesses Choate had no superior. His voice, with its controlled and musical tones, was reassuring, and he took care to treat each witness as if he were a gentleman. In cross-examination he did not, as some very good lawyers are accustomed to do, adopt a bullying attitude or resort to browbeating. Those who wished to tell the truth found him fair and considerate; but those who had something to conceal received no mercy, and he probed into the secret places of their hearts. On rare occasions he was outwitted in his examination. He was once pressing hard upon a sailor who had turned State's Evidence and had alleged that Choate's client instigated the theft of certain money. "Well," went on Choate confidently, "What did he say? Tell us *how* and *what* he spoke to you?" "Why," answered the witness in a loud voice, "he told us that there was a lawyer in Boston named Choate, and he'd get us off if they caught us *with the money in our boots!*"

Choate's reputation for wit and humor was bound to help him immensely with any jury. When he rose, everybody could be sure that something interesting was coming. His legal discussions were never so prolonged as to be tiring, and his grotesque exaggerations, his whimsical anecdotes, and his unusual illustrations helped to enliven even the arid places in his narrative. Carefully avoiding the dullness of formal logic, he won his way into the graces of the jury without their suspecting what was being done. The many stories that are related to him lose much because the tone and manner with which they were originally told cannot be reproduced,—for every good story is at least one-half in the personality of the teller. Once a lawyer interrupted him in the midst of a patent case to say, "Look here, there's nothing original in your patent; your client did not come by it naturally." Choate, surprised, looked up at his opponent. "What does my brother mean by *natur-*

ally?" he inquired suavely. "Naturally? We don't do anything naturally! Why *naturally* a man would walk down Washington Street with his pantaloons off!" Here the laughter which was produced obscured the point of the other lawyer's remark,—which was precisely what Choate intended it to do.

In the case of *Shaw* v. *Worcester Railroad*, already referred to, Choate, while he was stressing the point that the railroad company had no lookout at the crossing where Shaw was killed, burst out, "They say the engine driver was the lookout. The engine driver the lookout! Why, what was he doing at this moment of transcendent interest? What was the lookout doing? Oiling his pumps, they say,—*oiling his pumps*, gentlemen of the jury! A thing he had no more business to be doing than he had to be *writing an epic poem of twenty-four lines!*" This ridiculous association of widely remote ideas is strongly reminiscent of Sergeant Buzfuz's famous speech at the trial of *Bardell* v. *Pickwick*, and the intentional burlesque, with its appeal to the sense of humor of the jurymen, helped undoubtedly to gain their verdict.

It was in the same case that Choate scored when one of the witnesses for the defense, Colonel Rice, testified that the wagon containing Shaw came on at a steady pace until it was close by the track, where the horse

[185]

stopped. The witness continued, "Yes, the horse stopped; the horse thought"—"Wait a moment," interposed Choate, addressing the Bench. "May it please your Honor, Homer tells us in his *Iliad* of the dogs' dreams; but I prefer better authority than Colonel Rice's for the horse's thoughts. I object to the statement."

Let us picture for ourselves the scene in the courtroom on the morning when the great advocate is to argue an important case. Haggard and gray after a night of final preparation, his sad and weary eyes framed in bluish circles, he slips unobtrusively into his place, and takes a pile of documents from his green bag. As he arranges them on the desk, the spectators notice his quaint costume. Although it is midsummer and the weather is dry, he wears upon his feet clumsy heavy rubber overshoes. Around his neck is a kind of stole, like the section of a sheep's fleece, and his body is wrapped in several overcoats of different colors, the outside one being a coarse and heavy garment, which slips off easily when he desires. Sitting at his desk, his long bony fingers twitching nervously, his feverish eyes wandering from one corner to another, he looks like a runner awaiting the starter's gun. The crier finishes his business, the jurymen are in the box,—Rufus Choate's rapid scrutinizing glances have not missed them, we may be sure,—and the Court gives the signal for the opening. Then, while a hum of excitement travels through the crowd, he strips for action by pulling off two or three coats, pushes the table away in front of him in order to get space to move, and begins in a calm voice, "May it please your Honor and Gentlemen of the Jury" . . . The argument is on!

He is in a state of nervous agitation, keenly susceptible to all sounds and motions in the courtroom. Once, while he was addressing a jury, a woman rose and went out, with some rustling of silk petticoats. "Did you notice it?" asked some one after the trial was over. "Notice it!" he replied, "I thought forty battalions were moving." . . . But he does not seem on this occasion to be excited. With studied coolness he pays compliments to the judge and to the jury, setting everybody at ease. Then he turns casually to the pile of papers, of various sizes and shapes, on the desk before him,— papers decorated with that inimitable and illegible scrawl which, according to one of his students, could not be deciphered without the aid of a pair of compasses and a quadrant. Slowly he warms to his subject, bringing his listeners by degrees up to his own heat, until they partake of his fervor and are in harmony with him. It is as if they were magnetized by contact with some amazingly powerful electrical force. His flow of language becomes more rapid as he dashes on,—one short-hand reporter gave him up in despair, saying, "Who can report chain lightning?"

At last he is going at top speed, turning now to the judge and now to the jury, picking up torn fragments of foolscap and tossing them away, making remarks to his associate counsel, talking always at some person or group of persons, waving his arms or swaying from side to side in the overflow of his emotion, sometimes shaking his whole frame as if to generate new enthusiasm and then rushing tempestuously on. The audience is thrilled. He has communicated his enthusiasm to his hearers. The jury are in the hollow of his hand. . . . And then suddenly the climax comes! With his standing collar wilted and his cravat awry, he sinks, exhausted, into his seat, aware for the first time of his aching head and his muscles limp from fatigue. Those who have heard him draw near to offer their congratulations, feeling that he may, perhaps, never speak again after this tremendous demonstration of energy. He leaves the hall in moody loneliness, as if he had no vitality whatever to sustain him, as if the battery were fully depleted. He has been vibrating for half a day with nervous energy; now he is paying the inevitable penalty. From exaltation to depression, from confidence to despair,—such are life's rapid transitions!

[188]

But when the burden was removed from his shoulders, he was soon able to forget it. A night's rest, and he was ready again for action. "When I have once argued a case," he told Whipple, "and it is settled, I am done with it. I cast it forcibly out of my mind, and never allow it to trouble my peace. I should go mad if I allowed it to abide in my thoughts." His recuperations were so rapid as to make it appear as if he owned some magical rejuvenator. One trial was hardly over before he was eager for the next, prepared to give to it the same enthusiasm and concentration which had been accorded to the one of yesterday. He indulged in no regrets or rejoicings. He had done his best, and he did not choose to dwell in the past. It was the future, with its new and unfathomed problems, which interested him.

"When a case has gone against me," he once said to a friend, "I sometimes feel like the Baptist clergyman who was baptizing in winter a crowd of converts through a large hole made in the ice. Brother Jones disappeared after immersion, and did not reappear; he had probably drifted ten or fifteen feet from the hole, and was vainly gasping under ice as many inches thick. After pausing a few minutes, the minister said, 'Brother Jones has evidently gone to kingdom come,—bring on the next.' Now I am not unfeeling; but after all has been done for a client that I can do,—and I never spared myself in advocating his legal rights,—the only thing left for me is to dismiss the case from my mind, and to say with the Baptist brother, 'bring on the next!' "

Such was Rufus Choate's professional life,—every few days a new part to play, a new battle to win, each different from the one before it. It was exciting while it lasted, but no human organism could stand the strain very long. There came a time when the mechanism was worn out, when the battery could no longer be recharged. But long before that moment, Rufus Choate had made his place in history as the greatest of American advocates before a jury.

CHAPTER IX

In the Public Eye

*A*LTHOUGH, after leaving the United States Senate in 1845, Rufus Choate never again sat in a legislative body, his position was such that his views on public questions were sought, and he could not avoid stating his opinions on controversial issues. Whenever there was a Whig gathering of any importance, Choate was implored to address it. In 1848, after Webster had declared General Zachary Taylor's nomination one "not fit to be made," the Whigs turned to Choate, who helped them out by speaking before large mass meetings in Worcester and Salem, being present in the latter city when the ladies of Salem, with an unconsciously ironic gesture, presented to the local Whig Club a banner showing General Taylor giving relief to a wounded Mexican, with the words underneath,—"HONOR—PATRIOTISM—HUMANITY."

The climax of the campaign for him was reached in a speech which he made at Brookline. Fortunately we have a picturesque description of his mood just

before he addressed the audience, a mood that is typical
of him.

He had been a week preparing his oration, and was well-
nigh used up. He got into the coach, his locks dripping with
dissolved camphor, and complained of a raging headache. He
clutched his temple with his hand, and leaned his head on my
shoulder, to see if he could not, by reclining, find ease. Just
as we touched the Mill Dam, the evening moon poured her
level rays over the beautiful waters of the Back Bay, and filled
the coach and atmosphere with dreamy light. The scene instantly revived him. He put his head out of the coach window, and was absorbed with the sweetness of the view. The
sight of the still waters, moon-lighted, seemed to drive away
his pain, and he struck into his old rapture. In the hall where
he spoke, he was in his very best mood, both mind and body
seeming to be on wings.

Such spectacular contrasts are frequent enough in
the career of Rufus Choate. Even when he was most
depressed, there was some store of hidden nerve force
upon which he could draw to sustain him through an
oratorical ordeal. Moreover he was really devoted to
the cause. When Taylor defeated Lewis Cass so de-
cisively, Choate, with amusing exuberance, said to a
friend,—"Is it not sweet? Is it not sweet? The whole
country seems to me a garden to-night, from Maine to

New Orleans. It is fragrant all over, and I am breathing the whole perfume."

Choate's prominence at the Bar inevitably brought with it offers of various positions, nearly all of which he courteously declined. After the death, in 1848, of Justice Story, who had been Dane Professor in Harvard Law School, the members of the Harvard Corporation made an ambitious effort to secure Rufus Choate in his place. Realizing that it would be impossible to persuade him to abandon his practice altogether, they evolved a plan by which Choate could be absent in Washington during the entire session of the United States Supreme Court, from early December to the middle of March. During the remainder of the two terms at the Law School he could lecture to the students. . . . It was stipulated, however, that he should forego all jury trials and all other cases except an occasional argument before the Supreme Judicial Court, in Boston. It was considered essential that Choate should reside in Cambridge on account,—to quote the words of Chief Justice Shaw,—"of the influence which his genial manners, his habitual presence, and the force of his character would be likely to exert over the young men drawn from every part of the United States to listen to his instructions." Choate was touched by the compliment and did not immediately decline the offer; but a

[193]

week later he informed Shaw that he could not accept. It will easily be understood that Choate, who loathed being tied down by routine and whose passion was jury practice, would have been unhappy in a professorial chair, even at Harvard.

At about this time also he declined a seat on the Supreme Bench of the Commonwealth, offered him by Governor George N. Briggs. In September, 1851, after the death of Judge Levi Woodbury, Webster wrote President Fillmore suggesting that Rufus Choate was the ideal man for the vacant place as Justice of the Supreme Court of the United States, but adding that Choate would not serve. Choate himself shortly corroborated Webster's statement, and the position was filled by the appointment of Benjamin R. Curtis. Choate's reasons for declining the honor were mainly two: first, a desire to make for his family a larger financial income than he could receive as judge; and second, a conviction that he was not temperamentally suited to wear the ermine. He had so long accustomed himself to the modes of thought peculiar to the special pleader that he believed himself to be almost incapable of weighing evidence impartially,—and he may have been right.

In the early summer of 1850, Choate, aware that he was worn out by his unremitting toil of previous

[194]

years, sailed for Europe with the Honorable Joseph
Bell, a well-known New Hampshire lawyer who had
married Mrs. Choate's sister. It was Choate's only trip
abroad,—a hurried period of travel through England,
Belgium, France, Germany, and Switzerland, such as
school teachers take to-day during their vacations. He
seems to have found much to divert him in the sights
which he saw and the people whom he met, among
whom were Macaulay and Guizot. But even after
seeing Westminster Abbey and the British Museum, his
mind was still on his practice, and he wrote,—"I wish
J. would ascertain the latest day to which my causes in
the S. J. C. can be postponed, and write very particularly which must come on, and at what times, doing his
best to have all go over till October, if possible." When
he was not in motion or occupied in sight-seeing, his
thoughts reverted to his pending cases, and he longed
for home. How could a man of that temperament get
any rest, in Europe or anywhere on earth?

Choate was a keen observer, and, in his *Journal*,
commented freely on what he had seen. He was much
interested in the procedure of the English courts, and
found no English advocate who, in action, impressed
him by "point, force, language, power; still less, eloquence or dignity." He caught his first glimpse of
Paris "at nine in the evening, by moonlight," and

[195]

viewed it "with any feeling but that of disappointment." But he returned with a decided conviction that his own country was best, after all. He made a memorandum in Switzerland,—"The enjoyment of an American of refined tastes and a spirit of love of man is as high as that of a European of the same class. He has all but what visits will give him, and he has what no visits will give the other." Again he asked himself,—"What is it worth to live among all that I have seen?" and gave his own answer,—"I think access to the books and works of art is all." After he had visited Cambridge, he grew more enthusiastic, and could speak in praise of "that marked, profound English policy, which in all things acquires but keeps,—and binds the ages and generations by an unbroken and electric tie." But we cannot help feeling that he was glad to embark on the ship for America, and that, when he reached Boston in September, he was overjoyed to be back once more at the yellow pine desk, interviewing prospective clients and preparing for his cases in court.

When Rufus Choate returned to the United States, Zachary Taylor was dead and Millard Fillmore was President, Daniel Webster was Secretary of State, and the nation was in a mood of intense excitement, both North and South, over the so-called Compromise Measures of 1850. Before Choate sailed, he had, of course, read Webster's Seventh of March Speech, in which that sagacious statesman had advocated concessions to the South in order to save the Union,—a policy of which Choate thoroughly approved and which to many students of that period to-day seems to have been far-sighted. When, therefore, a "Constitutional Meeting" was called on November 28, in Faneuil Hall, Choate consented to be the principal speaker. John C. Warren was the President, and Choate was preceded by Judge Benjamin R. Curtis, B. F. Hallett, and S. D. Bradford. In his brilliant address, after emphasizing the dangers that then threatened the Union, Choate urged his hearers "to suppress or mitigate the political agitation of slavery." He insisted that the Compromise Measures gave the whole victory to neither side; he stated his belief that the Fugitive Slave Law,—the feature of the Compromise to which abolitionists most objected,—was not only constitutional but necessary; and he reiterated his conviction that the Constitution did not give to Congress the power "to intermeddle by law with slavery within its States." "Our moral duties," he said, "not at all less than our political interests demand that we accept this compromise, and that we promote the peace it is designed to restore."

There were many well-intentioned citizens of Massachusetts,—men like Whittier and Garrison and

Sumner,—who did not share Choate's enthusiasm for Webster's actions and who did their best to make things hot for the Marshfield statesman. In April, 1851, while the Secretary of State was on a brief visit to his home, plans were made for a public reception to him in Faneuil Hall, with an address of welcome by Rufus Choate. It was a fitting compliment to a great man whose career on this earth was almost ended. But, after the meeting had been publicly announced, the Mayor and Aldermen of Boston refused the use of the Hall for that purpose, giving as an excuse the fact that they had just declined to allow Wendell Phillips and the abolitionists to gather there, and could not, therefore, open it to Webster and his supporters. Choate was highly indignant and wrote Webster that the insult of the city fathers did not represent the sentiment of the citizens of Boston; unfortunately when Fletcher Webster brought this letter to Marshfield, his father looked at it and said, "Tell Mr. Choate to write better; his handwriting is barbarous. I cannot read a single word. . . . Tell Mr. Choate to go to a writing-school and take a quarter's lessons." When, a few days later, the Common Council of the City of Boston invited him to meet them in the historic building, Webster replied in a letter in which he used the famous sentence,— "Nor shall I enter Faneuil Hall, till its gates shall be thrown open, wide open, not 'with impetuous recoil—grating harsh thunder' but with 'harmonious sound, on golden hinges moving,' to let in, freely and to overflowing, you and your fellow-citizens, and all men, of all parties, who are true to the Union as well as to Liberty." Peter Harvey was entrusted with this letter, with instructions to show it to Choate and ask him to alter it or amend it before it was despatched. When Choate had read it, he looked at Harvey with astonishment, "I amend a letter of Mr. Webster's! I should as soon think of amending the Acts of the Apostles! The letter is perfect,—nobody else could write such a letter!"

In the following May came the sequel, when Webster, who had just recovered from a serious carriage accident, agreed, somewhat imprudently, to appear once more in Faneuil Hall. He was given a tremendous ovation, and Rufus Choate, who introduced him, referred happily to the gates of Faneuil Hall as open now,—"Aye, and on golden hinges turning!" Webster found it "an occasion altogether agreeable."

Meanwhile Choate had been busy with plans for the presidential campaign of 1852. A Whig Convention in Massachusetts, held on November 25, 1851, adopted an address to the people of the United States, written by Edward Everett and nominating Webster for the Presidency. At this gathering, Choate made the principal

[199]

speech, thrilling the crowded hall with his glorification of Webster and defending him against the angry and slanderous attacks of his enemies.

The Whig Party met on June 18, 1852, in Baltimore, for its last great national convention, and Rufus Choate, of Massachusetts, was a delegate, bent on forcing the nomination of Daniel Webster as the Whig standard-bearer. In the light of future events, we can see that Webster, if he had been named, would have been defeated; as a matter of fact, he did not live even until election day. But Rufus Choate had no supernatural power of divination. He had just one aim,—to place in the White House the leader who seemed to him best qualified to preserve the Union through a period of crisis. The hall was hot and stuffy, and the delegates were not disposed to tolerate long speeches. But there was one man to whom they listened gladly,—and that man was Rufus Choate.

His opportunity came when, after two days of routine organization, a party platform had been brought in binding the Whigs to the Compromise of 1850. In the late afternoon, Choate arose to address the throng of delegates. In substance, his speech was an earnest appeal to his fellow Whigs to declare without reservation that the further agitation of the subject of negro servitude should, in the future, be excluded from national politics. Speaking of the Compromise Measures of 1850, he said, "I rejoice that the healthy morality of the country, with an instructed conscience, void of offense toward God and man, has accepted them." . . . It was long the fashion for Northern historians, still animated by the violent prejudices of the Civil War, to denounce such men as Webster and Cushing and Choate for their unsympathetic attitude towards abolition and abolitionists, and even to intimate that they were cowards, afraid to face the slavery issue. What had Choate to fear? There was no office which he would not have refused, no political ambition which he desired to gratify. Making every effort to be fair-minded and think in terms of the entire country, South as well as North, he deplored an agitation which threatened to destroy the Union which he loved. What he did not fully realize was the destructive violence of the animosities which had been aroused, and which could not be calmed by reason or discussion, but could be eradicated only by the pouring out of blood, at a stupendous cost of treasure and human lives.

At the conclusion of his speech, Choate was wildly applauded. Then the irrepressible Botts, of Virginia, rose to complain that Choate had cast imputations on the character of General Winfield Scott and had praised Daniel Webster. In reply, Choate uttered one para-

[201]

graph which stands out in the history of American oratory,—a panegyric on Webster:

I am suspected of having risen to pay a personal compliment to that great name with which I confess my heart is full to bursting, because I stand here, according to my measure, to praise and defend the great system of policy which the unanimous judgment of this Convention has approved, or is about to approve and promulgate. Ah, Sir, what a reputation that must be,—what a patriotism that must be,—what a long and brilliant series of public service that must be,—when you cannot mention a measure of utility like this but every eye spontaneously turns to, and every voice spontaneously utters, that great name of Daniel Webster!

The scene which followed this impassioned outburst was the great moment of the Convention. Bouquets were thrown at the speaker, and he was cheered until tired throats could shout no more. Probably it was Choate's finest personal triumph. The platform which he advocated was adopted by a vote of 227 to 66. Even Choate's persuasive powers, however, were insufficient to procure the nomination of Daniel Webster. The Massachusetts delegates gave a dinner to those from the Southwest, hoping to induce them to vote for their candidate. Choate, on that evening, had gone to bed with one of his devastating headaches, and, when one of his friends came to him and begged him to speak, he replied, "I can't do it. I am too ill to hold up my head. I haven't strength to say a word." Nevertheless, to help his friend Webster, he did get up, sat at the dinner table without touching a morsel of food, and then spoke for fifteen minutes with a splendor which dazzled the audience. There was a noisy demonstration, when men broke their wine glasses, beat upon the table with their knives, and jumped upon chair and benches to shout in a kind of summer madness. . . . But mere noise does not mean votes. There was never a time when crowds would not cheer themselves hoarse for Webster and for William Jennings Bryan,—but neither could win the Presidency. When the balloting began, the vote for Webster was never more than thirty-two, all from New England. On the fifty-third trial, the choice fell on General Scott,—a man who, from every point of view except possibly that of a soldier, was Webster's inferior.

Returning fatigued and depressed from Baltimore, Choate went to the University of Vermont in August to deliver a Phi Beta Kappa Address and from there made a short excursion to Quebec and Montreal, from which he came back to his practice with renewed vigor. On October 24, Daniel Webster died, his last days saddened by his failure to secure the Whig nomination, and Choate went to Marshfield to attend the funeral. With other eminent lawyers, he addressed the United States

Circuit Court four days later, when resolutions were submitted expressing the condolences of the Suffolk Bar; and, declining other similar requests, he accepted an invitation from Dartmouth College to deliver a more extended eulogy in the following year.

Rufus Choate took no active part in the campaign of 1852. If Webster had lived, he would probably have voted for Franklin Pierce, but this Choate could not do. In a letter sent in late October to the President of the Boston Young Men's Whig Club, he came out publicly for Scott, mainly because, with all his weakness, he was the Whig candidate. "It is quite needless to say," he concluded, "that I shall vote for the regularly nominated Whig ticket of electors. He,—the best beloved, the most worthy,—is in his grave. Duty subsists, still and ever, and I am entirely persuaded that duty requires of me this vote." Doubtless he had no illusions as to Scott's chances; and, when Franklin Pierce was triumphantly elected, Choate could have shed very few tears.

On January 14, 1853, Rufus Choate's mother, well over eighty years old, died at the family home in Essex. For forty-five years she had survived her husband, existing only in the happiness of her children, and taking pride in the achievement of her distinguished son. It was time for her, after "life's fitful fever," to find rest in the shaded cemetery within sight of the ocean which she had watched from childhood to old age.

Early in the same year, Choate accepted from Governor John H. Clifford an appointment as Attorney General of the Commonwealth, an office which he accepted mainly because it enabled him to avoid being retained in cases arising from the liquor law of 1852. It has been said that the prosecutions undertaken by him were not generally successful, and he found so many details of the position distasteful and irksome that he was glad to retire at the end of his term.

During the spring and summer Choate performed an important service to his native state by sitting as a member of the Constitutional Convention called in Boston on May 3. It was composed of some of the wisest and most patriotic citizens of Massachusetts,—such leaders as Charles Sumner, Henry Wilson, Marcus Morton, Henry L. Dawes, Richard Henry Dana, Jr., George S. Boutwell, George N. Briggs, Nathaniel P. Banks, George S. Hillard, Benjamin F. Butler, Charles Allen, and Rufus Choate. Choate was appointed a member of the Committee on the Judiciary,—a position for which he was perfectly fitted,—and spoke frequently on the floor of the Convention, especially in opposition to the not inconsiderable portion of the members who favored an elective judiciary.

[205]

His most splendid contribution, without a doubt, was made on July 14, when he spoke on Judicial Tenure. Any one who has lived in New England knows how wiltingly oppressive a July day can be. It was like a fiery furnace in the Hall of Representatives where the sessions were being held. No breath of air was stirring except from the waving palm leaf fans of the delegates; yet Rufus Choate, suffering from illness and looking utterly wretched, rose and delivered an address which, in its reported form, covers twenty-six large pages in Brown's *Life* and took more than two hours to speak. On that day he was provided with a bottle of bay rum with which he frequently bathed his head, and, when he gesticulated violently, the drops were thrown on his neighbors. He held the rapt attention of what has been called "the ablest body of men ever assembled in Massachusetts." It was, broadly considered, a carefully built argument against the election of judges by popular vote and against any limitation of their tenure of office. Opening with a description of the ideal judge as a man not only learned in the law but fair-minded and possessing the confidence of the community, he went on to prove that the existing system of executive appointment during good behavior was likely, on the whole, to be better than any other. He examined carefully the experience of British and American courts.

[206]

He pointed out that the principle of executive appointment had worked well in Massachusetts, and that there was no imperative demand for a change. And then he ended with a peroration, the imagery for which was drawn from remembrances of his boyish days on the Essex County coast:

Sir, the people of Massachusetts have two traits of character,—just as our political system in which that character is shown forth has two great ends. They love liberty; that is one trait. They love it, and they possess it to their heart's content. Free as storms to-day, do they not know it, and feel it,—every one of them, from the sea to the Green Mountains? But there is another side to their character, and that is the old Anglo-Saxon instinct of property; the rational and the creditable desire to be secure in life, in reputation, in the earnings of daily labor, in the little all which makes up the treasures and the dear charities of the humblest home; the desire to feel certain when they come to die that the last will shall be kept, the smallest legacy of affection shall reach its object, although the giver is in his grave; this desire, and the sound sense to know that a learned, impartial, and honored judiciary is the only means of having it indulged. They have nothing timorous in them, as touching the largest liberty. They rather like the exhilaration of crowding sail on the noble old ship, and giving her to scud before a fourteen-knot breeze; but they know, too, that, if the storm comes on to blow, and the masts go overboard, and the gun-deck is rolled under water, and the lee-shore edged with foam, thunder under her stern, that the sheet-anchor and best bower then are everything! Give them good ground tackle, and they will carry her round the world and back again, till there shall be no more sea.

Read this aloud to-day, giving full voice to each sonorous syllable, and you cannot help being stirred by the richness of the language. How much more impressive must it have been in that July of 1852, when Rufus Choate, as he uttered those noble, last phrases amid the profound silence of the assemblage, sank down, pressed his hand to his head, all crumpled, disheveled, and exhausted, and staggered down the aisle to the door, on the arm of Henry Wilson! Drawing around him the two or three wraps with which he was always provided, he was driven off to his home, leaving an audience still marveling over his eloquence. The plan to establish an elective judiciary was successfully opposed, but Choate and his friends were not able to block a proposal to limit the tenure of office for judges to ten years. Fortunately in some respects, the labors of the Convention were wasted, for the Constitution, when submitted to the people, was rejected.

In the very midst of this Convention, and while hampered by other business, Choate was spending spare hours in "trying to get a few things together to say at Dartmouth College in relation to Mr. Webster," and on

August 27, at Hanover, he delivered his *Eulogy on Daniel Webster*, perhaps the most truly eloquent of all his public addresses. It is not astonishing that, after these unusual exertions, he was under a physician's care and had, for the first time in his life, an illness which caused his friends real anxiety. He wrote on November 13, "I have come quite near being placed among the *Emeritus* Professors in the great life university, that reserved and lamentable corps, whose 'long day is done,' and who may sleep." He did recover, however, but got up from his bed with injunctions "to do but little, nor do that little long, at a time." The consequent necessary alteration in his habits set him thinking, for he had never before been positively curbed in his activities. He was able to goad himself through what he described to his son, Rufus, as "a very fatiguing winter," and his regular law work went on with its customary success through 1854. But, almost without knowing it, he had passed the climacteric and was on the downward slope. Never again would he be capable of the extraordinary achievements which he had accomplished in his prime.

An accident, apparently trivial at first, definitely marked the coming of old age. While he was trying a case at Dedham, he hit his knee against the corner of a table. Inflammation of the joint unluckily supervened, and he had to submit to a minor surgical operation. He

took ether,—something of an adventure in those days,—
and told one of his friends that it was all very pleasant
until the moment when he utterly surrendered consciousness,—"then death itself could not have been more
awful." He wrote on June 29, 1855,—"I am slowly
getting well,—nothing remains of it all but a disabled
knee, and that is slowly getting well too." But he was
confined to his room for several months, and, when he
did reappear, hobbling on two crutches, some of the old
energy and magnetism were gone, and he never fully
regained it. It was as if, in that period of suffering,
some vitalizing fluid had been drained from his system,
leaving him looking superficially quite himself, but
without the intensity of action for which he had once
been so remarkable. Acquaintances, watching him as
he crossed Boston Common, said from their club windows, "Rufus Choate isn't what he was! He's getting
old!"

As he lay convalescing, Rufus Choate was pondering on some of the most baffling political problems that
he had ever been obliged to face. The Kansas-Nebraska
Act, signed in May, 1854, and definitely abandoning the
principles of the Missouri Compromise of 1820, had
established a new doctrine,—that of "popular sover-
eignty,"—and had compelled Choate to revise some of
his opinions. At first he had not been in sympathy with

Douglas's proposal, but he later was won over to that policy, chiefly for practical reasons. Meanwhile he recognized that the Whig Party, which he had helped to build up twenty years before and of which he had been a conspicuous leader, was moribund, if not defunct. Writing to a Whig Convention on October 1, 1855, he discussed the situation unreservedly. In Massachusetts, the so-called American Party, the members of which styled themselves "Know Nothings," based principally upon opposition to alien elements in our politics, was rapidly gaining strength and had shown amazing power at the polls; the Democratic Party was, of course, still in existence; and the newly-formed Republican Party was winning adherents from Whigs, Free Soilers, and Abolitionists. There had been strange moments when Choate was drawn towards the American Party, and he once told Parker that "the Know Nothing Party is the one for every young man to join who has any hopes." But in the October letter he assumes that loyal Whigs will not join either the American or the Democratic Parties; and he then proceeds to show that Whigs cannot consistently become Republicans. In conclusion, he used memorable words, reminiscent of the noble Websterian tradition which Choate was perpetuating,—"We join ourselves to no party that does not carry the flag and keep step to the music of the Union."

[211]

What Rufus Choate was almost pathetically seeking was a place in some party which could speak in terms of the nation as a whole,—not of one section, or one social class, or one creed or color. On October 31, 1855, he had an opportunity, before a densely packed audience of Whigs in Faneuil Hall, to make his position even more clear. After declaring that he and his friends would remain, for the present, Whigs, he went on particularly to denounce the newly formed Republican Party,—"the party of the sections,"—which he described as "an organization of all the people of the Free States, if they can get all, if not, majorities of all, into a political party proper, to oppose the whole people of all the Slave States, organized into just such another association upon the single, but broad and fertile topic of slavery." "I resist," he said, "and deprecate the mere attempt to form the party. I don't expect to live to see it succeed in its grasp at power. I am sure I hope I shall not, but I see the attempt making. I think I see the dreadful influence of such an attempt. That influence I would expose. Woe! Woe! to the sower of such seed as this!" He closed with a stirring eulogy of Webster, the greatest of the Whigs, who, he declared, could never have abandoned himself to "the gloomy enterprise of sectionalism."

The critical moment arrived in 1858, when Rufus

Choate, a Whig, had to make his choice among Fremont, the Republican, Fillmore, the American,—or Know Nothing,—and Buchanan, the Democrat. There was no one of the three which he liked unreservedly. From the first appearance of the Republican Party, however, he had opposed its tenets, and he told Parker in July, 1858, that "the Fremont party was a sectional, anti-Union party, and nothing should be undone to defeat it." As for the Know Nothings, Choate had prescience enough to see that their numbers were diminishing and that they were as certainly doomed as the Antimasons had been two decades before. This left only the Democratic Party,—the party which he had opposed from the time of Jackson down to that of Franklin Pierce. In coming out publicly for Buchanan, Choate had nothing whatever to gain, and he had much to lose, for he was going against the dominant sentiment of his state. His thesis was, in essence, simple enough,— he preferred to endure slavery rather than to suffer the horrors of civil war. Of two evils, he chose what seemed to him the lesser. Many of his friends and associates,—men like Sumner in Massachusetts and Seward in New York,—had joined the Republicans. It required a high kind of moral courage for him to stand up boldly in 1858 and espouse the unpopular side in the controversy over slavery. Nothing but a strong feeling of patriotism could have led him,—sick man that he was,—to denounce fanatics like Garrison, who advocated "a dissolution of this blood-stained Union."

Rufus Choate could have refrained from expressing any opinion. Instead, regarding that policy as cowardice, he sent an open letter, dated August 9, 1856, to the Maine Whig State Central Committee, insisting that "the first duty of Whigs . . . is to unite with some organization of our countrymen to defeat and dissolve the new geographical party, calling itself Republican. . . . It would more exactly express my opinion to say that at this moment it is our only duty." The details of the argument need not be discussed. The pith of it came at the close, when Choate said, "The contest in my judgment is between Mr. Buchanan and Mr. Fremont. In these circumstances, I vote for Mr. Buchanan. . . . He seems at this moment, by the concurrence of circumstances, more completely than any other, to represent that sentiment of nationality,—tolerant, warm, and comprehensive,—without which, without increase of which, America is no longer America."

And so Rufus Choate, like Edmund Burke before him, allied himself, towards the close of his life, with a party the views of which he had hitherto repudiated. Like Burke, too, he would have argued that he was absolutely consistent, absolutely true to certain basic convic-

[214]

tions which were more important than superficial party
loyalty. Old party symbols and names and creeds were,
for the moment, to be disregarded; the really vital thing
for good citizens to do was to make sure that the Republicans did not win. Choate was fighting against
Destiny!

The most dramatic speech of the campaign was
made on October 28, in the manufacturing city of
Lowell. Five thousand people had forced their way
into the largest hall in the city, on the second floor of
an old brick building. While Benjamin F. Butler,
already well known as a Democratic politician, was
making a few preliminary remarks, there was a dull
rumble, and the floor apparently settled at least an inch
or two. Butler immediately quieted the frightened audience, assuring them that the supports of the building
would be at once inspected. Choate then stepped forward to be greeted by a tumult of applause. When he
had spoken about half an hour, there was another ominous cracking, and Butler left the platform to see what
was happening. A hasty examination showed him that
the entire floor was about to give way, and that the
slightest mass movement on the part of the throng above
him might bring the whole structure to the ground, with
frightful loss of life. Keeping cool, however, he returned, walked the length of the room down the aisle to

the platform, and, without any expression of excitement, whispered to Choate, "If I can't get this crowd out quietly, we shall all be in hell in five minutes." Butler then mounted the stage, and, with admirable coolness, explained to those present that, though there was no imminent peril, it might be well for them to withdraw without haste. "This is the spot of greatest danger," he added, "and I shall remain here until all have gone out." Within five minutes the vast auditorium was empty as a shell, and a terrible catastrophe had been averted. Choate, who never lost his sense of humor, said to Butler as they emerged from the building,—"Brother Butler, when you told me that we should *all* be in five minutes in that locality unmentionable to ears polite, did you have the slightest idea of insinuating that both of us would go to the *same* place?" . . . He retired to his room at the hotel, but the crowd found him out and called for him so vociferously that, in spite of a raging headache, he addressed them for some time from a platform improvised in front of one of the windows.

Rufus Choate was, of course, assailed by those Whigs,—not few in number,—who had allied themselves with the Republicans. He received anonymous letters vitriolic with abuse; he was charged with the lowest motives, among them a desire to be revenged on Fillmore because the latter, while President, had refused to bestow upon Choate an office which he wanted; he was called a traitor to New England. His contemporary Caleb Cushing, who had been a Democrat since 1844, had run for Governor of Massachusetts on a Democratic platform, and had served as Attorney General under Franklin Pierce, had long since grown hardened to the insults of Massachusetts abolitionists; but Rufus Choate was going through a new and ugly experience. He was in every sense a generous, unselfish, and enlightened,—though possibly mistaken,—patriot; yet he was being called a renegade, and his honest motives were being misconstrued as if he were the vilest time-server. It has been his misfortune that the Republican policy prevailed and that Republican historians have written the story of that period. Choate's purposes, like Webster's, have been given wrong interpretations; but no fair-minded critic to-day can doubt, after an honest examination, that both men were at least as sincere and well-meaning as the most zealous abolitionist then within the boundaries of New England.

With the election of James Buchanan as President of the United States, the public life of Rufus Choate was virtually over. When Judge Curtis resigned from the Supreme Bench in 1857, Choate was mentioned as a possible successor, but he would not allow his friends to present his name. Probably he realized only too well

[217]

that his span of life was likely to be short; the same objections, furthermore, existed as in 1849. No office, however exalted, had for him then any temptations.

Some premonition of the future must occasionally have crossed his mind. Talking with his son-in-law, Edward Ellerton Pratt, in 1856, Choate, sitting on the rocks at Marblehead and looking out over the Atlantic, said,—"I shall not probably live to see it, but I fear there will ere long be a civil war between the North and the South." In an Independence Day Address, delivered at Tremont Temple in 1858, he made an inspiring plea for the Union. With studied casualness, he spoke of the dispute between the two sections as "this shadow that flits across our grasses and is gone, this shallow ripple that darkens the surface of our broad and widening stream." . . . It was more than that, as time was to show. Before the guns began firing, Rufus Choate was to be at rest in his grave at Mount Auburn. But his son, Captain Rufus Choate, Jr., was to contract at the front a disease which cost him his life; and his son-in-law and partner, Major Joseph M. Bell, was to be struck with paralysis as a consequence of his tireless labors on the staff of General Butler. The controversy was more than "this shadow that flits across our grasses." It was, though Rufus Choate was spared that knowledge, the ominous precursor of a furious and destructive storm.

[218]

CHAPTER X

The Orator and Scholar

*R*UFUS CHOATE lived in a period when formal oratory was much more highly esteemed in our country than it ever has been since. At the banquets of that copiously articulate time, a series of toasts numbering ten or twelve was not unusual; and people expected, on state occasions, to be edified by addresses of at least two or three hours in length. A preacher who did not let all the sand run through his hour-glass before he began his "Finally, my brethren," was not considered to have earned his salary. We, in reaction, have grown up with a distrust of affluence of speech; we regard a sermon more than twenty minutes long as intolerable; the average man is resentful when an after-dinner speaker, no matter who, attempts a serious discussion of any important topic.

In 1850, however, the genuine orator could find an intelligent audience for as long as he cared to declaim, and oratory itself was regarded as a fine art, well worth cultivating. As a platform speaker, Rufus Choate had

[219]

many rivals. In New England alone, there were Charles Sumner, Caleb Cushing, Edward Everett, Wendell Phillips, and the incomparable Webster,

"Whose words in simplest homespun clad,
The Saxon strength of Cædmon's had,
With power reserved at need to reach
The Roman forum's loftiest speech."

That he held his own in such a strenuous competition indicates that he possessed powers of the highest order. And that he did hold his own, even with the best at their best, there can be no doubt.

Fortunately we possess plenty of material on which to base an opinion. Some of his lectures have disappeared, including the famous one on *The Romance of the Sea*, delivered with great effect in his early Boston days and later stolen from his pocket in New York. It was said by one who heard it that "he seemed full of his wild subject, and swayed the audience with eloquence, as the storm sways the sea." But we do have some of his most popular addresses, corrected by his own hand, and from these we can get some of what the oratorical style of Rufus Choate was like.

Choate prepared himself patiently for every difficult ordeal. Like most really good public speakers he was always nervous before an important address, and he did not like to have his friends or students come to hear him. Extemporaneous discourse, he said, "must always be unequal and uncertain," and he enjoined a young admirer to write out his speeches in advance,—"that you may have, in speaking, the confidence and ease flowing from the certainty that you can't break down." "The more passionate parts," he added, "should be fully committed." Even when he was sure of having his manuscript before him, he memorized long passages so that they would flow trippingly from the tongue.

Upon the manner of delivery he bestowed no less attention. His own voice was deep and musical, of good carrying power and ample variety of tone. "Thrilling it can be as a fife, but it has often a plaintive cadence," said a keen critic. Once Choate, contemplating a bust of Cicero, observed that he "had the large mouth which eloquence almost always gives its possessor. Mr. Webster had a large mouth." Choate's mouth, too, was large, and his voice had volume enough to fill the most spacious halls. . . . But he did not depend altogether upon this natural endowment. Day after day he practiced intonation and expression, reading aloud from Burke, trying to make his voice "flexibly express all the changes of pitch and time appropriate to the fluctuations of the thought," and striving constantly to make his

[221]

tones "strong and full." In great moments his voice could be extremely loud, so that it could be heard in the corridors of the Court House. "Elocutionary training I most highly approve of," he said, and again and again he reiterated his conviction that good public speaking demands practice. "With fair natural gifts," he declared, "there's many a man who could make himself an orator." Even in posture and gesture he did not hesitate to pose before a mirror so that he might not do anything inappropriate. He always tried to talk directly to somebody in his audience, and sometimes would rush forward to the edge of the platform, turning his glance on a certain section of the hall until those upon whom he was gazing shrank back from his frenzied eyes.

The most conspicuous ornaments of Choate's library were the small bronze busts of Demosthenes and Cicero, two of the orators upon whom, according to his own confession, he modeled his style. Choate's advice to a young lawyer,—"Soak your mind with Cicero,"—was merely a statement of his own policy. He had high admiration for the "awful vehemence" of Demosthenes, and thought him the finest orator of ancient times. Among the moderns, he preferred Burke, whose style he never tired of praising. "Burke," he once said, "will live forever!"

A notable feature of Choate's style was his affinity

[222]

Rufus Choate, the Bronze Statue by French now standing in the Lobby of the Boston Court House.

for the right word. "You want a diction," he told a friend, "whose every word is full freighted with suggestion and association, with beauty and power." His vocabulary, through actual statistical testing, has been shown to be exceedingly large as compared with that of other writers and speakers. Once a member of the Boston Bar asked Judge Wilde whether he had heard that a new edition of Worcester's *Dictionary* had just been published, with a great number of additional words. "No, I have not heard of it," answered his Honor, "but, for God's sake, don't tell Choate." He once said that the Greek mind was "subtle, mysterious, plastic, apprehensive, comprehensive, available," and each one of these carefully chosen words connotes a definite and distinct quality.

In spite of an opinion sometimes expressed to the contrary, I am sure that Choate cared little for words just as words,—they must always reveal a thought. He made them his servile instruments, and was, as Whipple well maintained, "the least verbose of impassioned orators." His vocabulary was highly Latinized, and he enjoyed pronouncing a sonorous and unusual phrase. People who listened to him were likely to remember his language. Describing John Quincy Adams as a debater, he said, "He had an instinct for the jugular and the carotid artery as unerring as that of any

[223]

carnivorous animal." When one of his opponents in a case declared himself insulted at some of Choate's remarks, the latter disclaimed any intention of causing offense and added that he was unprepared for "such a tempestuous outbreak of extraordinary sensibility." While he was defending a divorce suit, and arguing against the probability of the guilt of his client, he said, alluding to her flirtation with the co-respondent,—"They were playful, gentlemen of the jury, not culpable. After the morning toil, they sat down on the haymow for refreshment, not for crime. There may have been a little youthful fondling,—playful, not amorous. They only wished to soften the asperities of hay-making!" The whimsicality of the final sentence, so characteristic of Choate's peculiar style, was bound to attract attention.

It is impossible to acquit Choate of the charge so frequently made that he used "flowery language." His critics, to support their position, quote sentences like the famous one from his *Eulogy on Harrison*, in which he refers to "New York, which with one hand grasps the golden harvests of the West, and with the other, like Venice, espouses the everlasting sea." But Burke himself employed abundant and gorgeous imagery, and Choate's imaginative mind also expressed itself naturally through the medium of tropes. A better illustration of

hís use of figurative language is a passage quoted by
Whipple in which Choate, describing the deterioration
of Marie Antoinette in prison, said, "The beauty of
Austria fell from her brow, like a veil, in a single
night." If his phrasing in this case was colored by his
intense emotion, it was because he himself was something of a poet although he spoke in prose. Furthermore he held the theory that such purple patches were
justifiable only when they were produced as the result
of strong feeling. And he could use figures of speech
which were more homely, as when he burst out, "What,
banish the Bible from our schools! Never, while there
is a piece of Plymouth Rock left large enough to make
a gun-flint of!"

The most valid criticism of all the oratory of the
"40's" and "50's" is that it is made up of "words, words,
words," that it is so patently artificial as to violate the
canons of good taste. Choate would not have been the
child of his age if he had not occasionally indulged in
inflated bombast about America and "the land of the
free." What redeems him is his obvious sincerity. His
somewhat florid language was actually the product of
his fiery enthusiasm. A very sound judge said of him,
"Mr. Choate was no doubt rich and exuberant in his
style, but who would not prefer the leap of the torrent
to the stagnation of the swamp?"

[225]

One of the best of his popular lectures,—as distinguished from those on political occasions,—was delivered on November 18, 1844, before the Mercantile Library Association, on the somewhat formidable subject *The Power of a State Developed by Mental Culture*. Feeling it unnecessary to resort to buffoonery or trickery in order to arouse attention, he paid his audience the compliment of a carefully worked out development of the thesis that it was time for Massachusetts to seize and retain the intellectual leadership of the nation. With an earnestness which thrilled his hearers, he dwelt on the power of the brain:

> I say that there is not an occupation of civilized life, from the making of the laws and poems and histories, down to the opening of New Jersey oysters with a broken jack-knife, that is not better done by a bright than a dull man, by a quick than a slow mind, by an instructed man than a gross and simple man, by a prudent, thoughtful, and careful man than by a light and foolish one.

Public characters, he went on, are better fitted for their tasks by "profound and liberal studies,"—and he cited John Quincy Adams as an excellent example. Finally he urged Massachusetts and her citizens to win a position of marked and acknowledged "literary and intellectual lead." Probably it did not even occur to his

[226]

modesty that he himself was a shining example of what he expected Massachusetts to produce. In a generation which could boast of a Sumner, a Cushing, an Everett, a Holmes, a Whittier, a Longfellow, a Thoreau, a Lowell, a Wendell Phillips, and an Emerson, the Old Bay State had no reason to struggle for literary and intellectual leadership. It was already hers. The pity is that she has not been able to retain it!

It is unessential to dwell at any length on the many lectures which Rufus Choate delivered from time to time before legal, literary, and scholastic organizations. He was always in demand, and the people listened to him gladly whenever he could be induced to appear. But one great address cannot be left unmentioned,—the *Discourse Commemorative of Daniel Webster,* spoken on July 27, 1853, at Dartmouth College. Seldom in American history have the occasion, the place, and the man been more perfectly blended to make a noble oration. Choate's invitation had reached him almost a year in advance. As the moment approached, he toiled incessantly during the hours which he could snatch from his practice, for he was ambitious to do something worthy of the Webster whom he loved. When the day arrived, he was there to march with the procession from Dartmouth Hall across the green to the colonial church where, thirty-four years before, he had stood as a young

[227]

graduate about to die and said farewell to his classmates. The hall was full, of course, and at least one admiring auditor sat for three long hours in an uncomfortable position on one of the window sills listening entranced to words which he was able to remember sixty years after. At last Rufus Choate rose, one Dartmouth man speaking to other Dartmouth men about Dartmouth's greatest alumnus, amid scenes which both he and Webster had known,—"the same range of green hills yonder, tolerant of culture to the top, but shaded then by primeval forests, on whose crest the last rays of sunset lingered."

One of the nation's greatest orators was eulogizing another. . . .

Rufus Choate, who never did a poor piece of work in his life, measured up fully to the significant occasion. He had known Webster and his career intimately; he had followed his leadership and agreed with him in his political principles; he had loved him as a man and a friend,—and it was no perfunctory praise which he bestowed. It has been said that he was far from satisfied with the circumstances under which the address was spoken. He began late in the afternoon, when neither he nor the audience was fresh, and the shadows of evening were falling before he had done. . . . But no one noticed the passing of time, and those who heard him were agreed that it was his finest exhibition of forensic oratory.

Those who want to know exactly what Choate said can find the oration in printed form, for it has been frequently republished. It was long, covering sixty-six pages of about four hundred words each,—not far from 26,000 words,—and the mere speaking of it was a considerable physical and emotional accomplishment. It was, in its aim, a biography and an appreciation, covering every phase of Webster's vivid career. Choate dwelt with special stress on Webster's attitude towards the protective tariff, on his negotiation of the Ashburton Treaty, and on his policy with regard to slavery, and, in natural conclusion, defended the Seventh of March Speech as an utterance of far-seeing statesmanship. He spoke with peculiar emphasis of Webster's argument in the Dartmouth College Case; and it ought not to be forgotten that Choate, in quoting an account of it sent to him by Dr. Chauncy A. Goodrich, preserved for posterity Webster's peroration with its memorable sentence, "It is, Sir, as I have said, a small college; and yet there are those who love it." Had it not been for Choate, this utterance might have been lost in the "dark backward and abysm of time."

Then, while the audience sat quiet, some of them weeping and every one in sympathy with the speaker, he threw his manuscript to one side and closed with moving words:

But it is time that this eulogy was spoken. My heart goes back into the coffin there with him, and I would pause. I went,—it is but a day or two since,—alone, to see again the home which he so dearly loved, the chamber where he died, the grave in which they laid him. . . . The books in the library, the portraits, the table at which he wrote, the scientific culture of the land, the course of agricultural occupation, the coming-in of harvests, fruit of the seed his own hand had scattered, the animals and implements of husbandry, the trees planted by him in lines, in copses, in orchards, by thousands, the seat under the noble elm on which he used to sit to feel the southwest wind at evening, or hear the breathings of the sea, or the not less audible music of the starry heavens, all seemed at first unchanged. The sun of a bright day, from which, however, something of the fervors of mid-summer were wanting, fell temperately on them all, filled the air on all sides with the utterances of life, and gleamed on the long line of ocean. Some of those whom on earth he loved best, still were there. The great mind still seemed to preside; the great presence to be with you; you might expect to hear again the rich and playful tones of the voice of the old hospitality. Yet a moment more, and all the scene took on the aspect of one vast monument, inscribed with his name and sacred to his memory. And such it shall be in all the future of America.

In the *Eulogy on Webster* we find some of Choate's distinctive qualities strongly accentuated. He had always been fond of building up long sentences, phrase after phrase and clause after clause, as an architect would construct a Gothic cathedral; but there is one sentence in the *Eulogy*, beginning "Consider the work he did in that life of forty years," which is probably the longest ever spoken by human lips, including as it does approximately twelve hundred words, and which must have taken at least ten minutes to finish. It is really a comprehensive life of Webster, covering his public service from 1813 to 1852. At least one of those who heard it "wondered whether he could make port without a wreck of grammar and connection," but somehow he emerged triumphant, amid the applause of the crowded hall. The modulations and emphases of his voice, the logical evolution of one idea from another, the skilfully cumulative reasoning, all helped to make this complicated sentence lucid. There was, after all, no real obscurity, for the mind of the orator was always in control, dominating the shifts of thought and giving it a fundamental unity.

But Choate knew better than to tire his hearers by requiring too much of their attention. Now and then he gave them relief by a series of crisp, short sentences, which stood out by contrast with what had preceded them, and seemed to halt for a moment the onward sweep of his imagination. But, on this occasion, he

[231]

avoided many of the conventional devices of the orator. He used almost no gestures, stepping at intervals from side to side or slightly back and forth, evidently to relieve the muscular strain, but seldom even lifting his arms from his sides. He stood on the platform "in the majesty of calm," every fiber of his being concentrated on the expression of thought in speech. Not a smile passed across his usually mobile face during all those three hours. The *Eulogy* was indeed, as some one has said, "the utterance of a soul with sorrow laden."

Even in his last years, Rufus Choate did not abandon platform speaking. In 1856, he prepared a lecture on *The Old Age of the Poet Rogers*, a theme which allowed him to leave his law courts for a topic entirely literary. He worked over it with great care, and told Parker that there was hardly a sentence which he had composed without glancing into at least fifty books. . . . In the hall there were four thousand people, of whom one thousand had to stand. A contemporary newspaper account says that the speaker "held their rapt attention for an hour and a half, so that eyes were riveted as by magnetic polarity upon him, breath almost suspended to catch his slightest accent, and the whole solid mass, as still as death all the time, one or two fainting women being carried out without in the least distracting their fixed and fascinated gaze." This was

[232]

the effect which Choate produced talking, not on some matter of vital political interest, but on a subject dealing with one of the fine arts. He had an opportunity, towards the close, of defending his favorite, Walter Scott, against the depreciation of Carlyle. Then he burst out with an eloquence which dragged the great audience to its feet, as if "a vast wave of the united feeling of the whole multitude surged up under every one's arm-pits." Here was a leader of the Boston Bar, battling for his clients every day in court, wearing himself out before a jury, yet able, as an intellectual pastime, to prepare a lecture which would have been a credit to a professional literary critic, like James Russell Lowell. Such an achievement makes us forgive him for his remark in 1856 that Longfellow was a better poet than Tennyson!

That Rufus Choate had power as a writer is unquestionable, and he was not free from literary ambitions. "A book," he said in 1850, "is the only immortality." Once in his journal he wrote,—"Some memorial I would leave yet, rescued from the grave of a mere professional life, some wise, or beautiful, or interesting page,—something of utility to America, which I love more every pulse that beats." He might have become a really great historian, for he could have made the people and the incidents of past times seem very much alive.

[233]

. . . Yet, aside from his lectures, he left behind him almost no literary work. In 1845, when he had a few days of leisure, he commenced a translation of Thucydides, which he carried out through section LXXVI; and a small fragment still remains of a translation of Tacitus undertaken later in the same summer. We have a *Journal,* which he kept intermittently, and a diary of his travels in Europe. But these are inadequate evidence of what Choate could do. He once said, "When I get home, even if I have an hour or two to spare, my mind is torn in pieces by the jar of the day, and I cannot do more than get in the mood for composition before I find my time is up." Under the right conditions, he might have been an American Macaulay or Trevelyan.

By instinct, Choate was a scholar. "He should have been a Greek professor," said Richard Salter Storrs, "but he somehow wandered into the law." He had a passion for accuracy which made him kin with Bentley and Porson. In the few minutes which he spent daily on his Latin and Greek, he worked with lexicons and commentaries at his elbow, consulting each in turn, and he never dropped a disputed question until he had settled it to his own satisfaction. He even dared to quote the Latin classics to jurymen who could not understand a word, but who felt flattered at the compliment. He

[234]

studied German late in life and read extensively in the philosophy of that country. His knowledge of ancient literature was profound. Once, at an informal gathering in Washington, the perennial subject of the depravity of the younger generation came up for discussion. Webster maintained that the only remedy for the prevalent vice and folly among boys and girls was in early religious training and parental discipline. Then Choate, adopting a tone which is equally familiar to our time, pointed out that there always has been, and always will be, criticism of the younger generation by their elders; and, to prove his point, he quoted a Latin passage to show that, in the period of Trajan, precisely the same complaints were voiced,—*Statim sapiunt, statim sciunt omnia; neminem verentur, imitantur neminem, atque ipsi sibi exampla sunt,*—which, freely translated, runs,—"From their cradles they know all things,—they understand all things,—they have no respect for any person whatsoever,—and are themselves the only examples which they are disposed to follow." Thomas H. Benton, the redoubtable Senator from Missouri, who did not care much for Choate, thought this quotation too happy to be genuine and asked for the author. Choate promptly took from the shelves a copy of Pliny's *Letters* and pointed out the passage in Letter XXIII of the Eighth Book.

[235]

Nor was he less conversant with the English masterpieces. One anecdote, often repeated in garbled forms, tells of a dispute between Choate and Webster during the trial of William Wyman for embezzlement. At one point, when things seemed to be progressing very slowly, Webster solemnly passed to his opponent a slip of paper on which he had scribbled a couplet from Pope:

> Lo, where Mæotis sleeps, and softly flows
> The freezing Tanais through a waste of snows.

Choate scrutinized the verse carefully, wrote at the bottom the word "Wrong!" and then emended the couplet as it should properly be quoted:

> Lo, where Mæotis sleeps, and *hardly* flows
> The freezing Tanais through a waste of snows.

He handed this back with equal seriousness to Webster, who returned the note with the rejoinder, "Right!!" and the offer of a wager. A messenger was despatched for an edition of Pope. Having examined it and demonstrated that he was correct, Choate handed the volume to Webster, who, after he had looked up the reference, penciled on the title page the words, "Spurious Edition!" and returned it. During this controversy, every-

[236]

body in the courtroom believed that the learned counsel were differing on an important question of law.

In 1845, George W. Nesmith rode from Boston to Hanover with Judge Levi Woodbury, Webster, and Choate, in the same stagecoach. To while away the tedious hours, the men covered a wide field in their talk. Nesmith inquired of Choate what reading he had been doing, and the latter spoke of Milton's prose and poetry. Webster, always alert, then said, "As you are so recently out of Paradise, won't you tell us something about the talk that Adam and Eve had before the fall?" Choate asked, "Do you intend that to be a challenge?" "Yes," replied Webster, "I do." Choate then began unhesitatingly to recite long passages from the conversation between Adam and Eve; and Webster, not to be outdone, declaimed, in his sonorous voice, the debate between Gabriel and Satan, in Book VI of *Paradise Lost*. Both men found in literature an anodyne for the troubles and vexations of this world.

As an orator, few men have been more fortunately equipped than Rufus Choate. Lacking Webster's majestic and Olympian presence, he had a fire and dramatic quality which were ample compensation. His voice was melodious and rich; his articulation was clear; his gestures were in harmony with his speech. But he displayed, besides these physical qualifications, intellectual

[237]

and moral resources of the highest order, and a magnetism which drew everybody to him. Boutwell said that "the effect of his personal appearance, gestures, and electrical voice can never be comprehended by those who had not the fortune to see and to hear him." He had his imitators, but they showed "the contortions of the Sybil without any of the inspiration." It was his unique and engaging personality which made him a great orator,—perhaps the greatest that this country has ever known outside of Daniel Webster. And there were moments of inspiration in which not even Webster was his superior.

CHAPTER XI

What the Man Was Like

T HE Rufus Choate whom Bostonians knew in the "50's" was a tall, broad-chested, rather uncouth figure, with large feet, bony hands, and broad shoulders, his hair black, glossy, luxuriant, and curling, without any trace of gray, even towards the end of his life. His forehead was not high but wide, and he had very prominent eyebrows. Although he had been handsome as a youth, the wear and tear of his unreposing life had channeled his face with weird wrinkles; but he was still striking looking, and people gazed at him with interest as they passed him in the street. He was called, with some accuracy, "the handsomest homely man in the world." Strong and vigorous though he was and able to withstand physical fatigue better than most men, he had a sensitive nervous organization and he was constantly overtaxing his nerves, with the result that he was a martyr to violent headaches. When he was warned by a friend that his incessant labor was endangering his health, he said, "I have no alternative but the insane

[239]

asylum." He often rose from his sick-bed to address a jury, driven on by sheer force of will. During one case in 1845 he had such a vertigo that he was compelled to hold on to his table with both hands while he spoke for two long hours. During five minutes of recess, he slipped out to his office and swallowed an emetic; he then returned and finished his argument.

He knew nothing, of course, of the golf and tennis and bridge through which Boston attorneys to-day get their recreation. Rising before daylight in both summer and winter, he would make himself a cup of tea and then take a walk, getting back for an hour's work at his desk before breakfast. In the afternoon he was frequently seen striding across Boston Common, his high shoulders swaying from side to side, like the opposite bulwarks of a ship. . . . But he resorted to muscular exercise because he felt that he ought to do it for his health,—not because he really liked it. When he did go out on walks, he perspired freely, and he was inclined to measure the efficacy of his exertion by the amount of perspiration which it produced. The direct opposite of Webster, who loved fishing and hunting and all forms of outdoor sport, Choate was happiest indoors. He preferred Thucydides to Mount Monadnock and Burke to the ponds of Marshfield. Even when his legs were carrying him along the Boston streets from his office to the Athenaeum, his mind was back in the Age of Pericles or pondering on some engrossing problem of the law.

Choate's permanent residence in Boston after 1851 was in a house at 3 Winthrop Place, now the western end of Devonshire Street, in a locality which is certainly not to-day filled with fashionable homes. Choate purchased his house from the estate of William Ward, a Boston business man, who in turn had acquired it in 1846 from Isaac McLellan. When he first moved in, his books filled a front room over the parlor. Then, by degrees, they overflowed, until they occupied every nook and corner of the second story. Some one asked him, "How did you contrive to gain for yourself so large a part of the house?" "By fighting for it!" was the reply, in a jocular tone. Within reach of the sofa where he usually reclined were several movable stands packed with books, and he even kept volumes stacked under his bed. It was said that he possessed more than eight thousand books, and the catalogue of his private library printed for a sale held after his death enumerates 2,672 separate items, some of them rare and many of them beautifully bound. The auctioneers estimated that the original cost of the library must have been more than $40,000.

Choate's books were most of them adorned with

[241]

marginal notes, and the pages showed that they had been read. His was a "working library," containing all the standard sets and reference volumes that a student would be likely to require. They had been bought in many places. During his trip abroad, he spent $500 on books. He used to be observed on Saturday afternoons in the famous Cornhill bookstores, picking up one volume here and another there, and bearing them proudly off under his arm to be examined later. His tastes were eclectic, and it might almost be said that he liked anything in print. One shelf was devoted entirely to editions of the Greek Testament, in all bindings and sizes. Once, in Washington, Webster came into Choate's lodgings and was browsing around among the books. Suddenly he turned and, in a voice of preternatural solemnity said, "I observe, brother Choate, that you are true to your instincts in Washington, as at home,—seven editions of the Greek Testament, but not a copy of the Constitution!"

When his private library did not meet his needs, Choate had recourse to the Boston Athenaeum, a share in which he owned as early as 1839. In the old building on Pearl Street, and later in the more modern structure on Beacon Street,—built in 1849,—Choate was usually to be found in the late afternoon. The records of loans show that he read much in classical literature and in poetry, with a peculiar fondness for bound volumes of *Punch*.

In his own home Choate was no autocrat, but the household unquestionably was arranged for his convenience. With his children, he was playful and affectionate, and full of whimsical jocosities. Following the practice in his mother's house, he liked to have them with him on Saturday evening; and on Sunday night, after tea, he would gather with them around the piano and sing some of his favorite hymns. At breakfast he would read passages from the morning newspaper aloud and comment on them. He and Mrs. Choate lived very simply, never attempting to entertain on a large scale or to make a display. There was always money enough for comfortable quarters and wholesome food, but the enervating luxuries were ignored. As for what is known as "society," neither Mr. or Mrs. Choate had the slightest desire to be recognized by it. "Society is mere trifling," he once told Parker. "If genius and culture enter society, they throw off their character and bend to its rules." On rare occasions he would go to the theater to see some great actor or actress, like Edwin Booth or Fanny Kemble, and he sometimes entered the Boston Museum to listen to the fun of William Warren.

Towards every one, rich or poor, exalted or humble, Rufus Choate was courteous, even when his temper was being sorely tried. He was exceedingly generous and often made handsome presents to his friends. Once he wrote Dr. Adams,—"Having had a child born within a few days, I have thought I could do no honester thing than to send my minister a volume of poetry,—a *votive* volume, as Wordsworth might say. I shall be sorry if you happen to own the edition." With the note went a royal octavo edition of Wordsworth. As a host, he was invariably gracious, and he was especially considerate of those with whose opinions he was at variance. "He gave you a chair," said his pastor, Dr. Adams, "as no one else would do it. He persuaded you at his table to receive something from him in a way that nothing so gross as language can describe. He treated every man as though he were a gentleman; and he treated every gentleman almost as he would a lady." With all his excitability, he was good-humored and unruffled in temper. In his heart he hated bores,—"well-meaning men, deficient in quickness of apprehension and directness of insight,"—but he did not let them know it. Once on a hot day, when Choate was exhausted by a long courtroom address, a dull man buttonholed him in order to explain at length some perfectly obvious propositions. Choate listened patiently, without a murmur, until the end. But, after the bromidic gentleman had departed, he turned to a bystander and said, "What an excellent person that is! But don't you think he would be much better if he could tell in a quarter of a minute what he has consumed fifteen minutes in telling?" Choate never obtruded his superior intelligence, and he was completely without arrogance or pretense.

His tolerance of stupidity and his unwillingness to say harsh things of others were part of his character. Very rarely his patience would be exhausted. Once, when he had obtained a settlement for his client, an injured but not very amiable wife, he said, "The woman's a sinner too,"—and then immediately corrected himself by saying, "No, she's not a sinner, for she is our client, but she is certainly a most disagreeable saint!"

On one notable occasion which Whipple graphically describes, Choate, although he had a painful bilious headache, was almost dragged from bed by an aggressive Whig politician and compelled to go to Faneuil Hall to make a campaign speech. On the platform, the orator looked like a corpse, and he was, for once, quite out of temper. When he was introduced, he began,— "Mr. Chairman, when you called upon me and demanded that I should address the Whigs of Boston, I respectfully informed you that, owing to ill-health and the pressure of my professional engagements, it was utterly impossible for me to be present on this occasion,— and accordingly *here I am!*" As he proceeded, he

[245]

quoted long passages of Ciceronian Latin, turning each time deferentially to the Chairman, who, although an excellent business man, knew no Latin whatever, and introducing each quotation slyly with satiric phrase, such as "As you, Mr. Chairman, well remember," or "As you, Mr. Chairman, cannot have forgotten," or "As you, Mr. Chairman, doubtless recollect." At first the audience did not sense the complete absurdity of the situation, but soon the bewildered expression of the Chairman made it apparent, and, whenever Choate turned to him with a fresh quotation, the crowd applauded, until the victim of the joke was wholly discomfited.

Although Choate was uniformly gracious, he did not confide much in others, and he was not inclined to say much about himself. He seemed unreserved, but there were chambers in his soul which were always locked. He had no really intimate friends, and, although he was forever in the midst of his clients or of the members of his household, he seemed lonely and solitary. He loved and admired Daniel Webster, and the two men were often very close,—but between them there was always a touch of formality, quite natural when one considers the seventeen years difference in ages. With Charles Sumner he carried on a correspondence, even after their differing views on political questions had thrown them into opposing camps. Of his son-in-law and partner,

Joseph M. Bell, he was very fond, and the two were frequently on excursions together. During his serious illness in 1855, Edward Everett, whom he had known since his Harvard Law School days, called on him two or three times a week, and the two became very intimate. It was then that Choate said, "I love Everett more now and understand him better than I ever did before in my life." The two had many of the same tastes and opinions, and it was natural that they should be congenial. . . . But Choate's truest friends were his books! They could never disappoint or betray him, and they were always there when he came home, burdened with care, from his office. He said to Parker, "After a fortnight's trial of a vexing cause, beaten and dispirited, I have next morning taken up my classic or other books, and *in an hour* dispelled the cloud."

So far as any personal ambition was concerned, Rufus Choate seemed almost completely indifferent. Chandler, in a discriminating eulogy, once said, "Most of our race are looking forward to some especial and prospective benefit as a reward for present exertions. The desire of wealth, the love of power, official position, an old age of ease, the 'Sabine farm' in the distance,—these not seldom appear with considerable distinctness,—but not with him. He appeared to labor for the love of it." In money matters, he was exceedingly

[247]

generous. Any one of his acquaintances could borrow from him freely, and he never dunned anybody for a debt. Webster accepted loans from Choate, as he accepted them from all his friends, and Choate's hieroglyphic signature was often found at the banks on Webster's notes. Even in political contests, Choate declined all compensation for his expenses, and he lost thousands of dollars by neglecting to collect his fees as counsel. To Choate, money and position really seemed unimportant as compared with success in the law.

In a period when many public men were often seen intoxicated in public, Choate would never drink more than a glass or two of sherry or brandy,—and then only on special occasions. He neither smoked nor took snuff, and he was abstemious in his eating. "Hot water and tea," he said, "are the best stimulants for a speaker. They leave no sting behind." The extraordinary excitement under which he sometimes labored while conducting a case led to the legend that he was an opium eater, but there seems to be no evidence whatever for the conjecture. The stimulant for him was his own nervous system, which was never in a state of repose. Once when a friend of his took him driving and let the horse break into a fast trot, Choate said, putting out his hand, "I want you to drive me as slowly and as carefully as if I were a Methodist minister going to meeting." Now

[248]

and then, as an expression of feeling, he would swear, but his profanity was harmless, and he was far more likely to employ some unusual expletive, such as "I'm perfectly *flabbergasted*" or "I'll eat all the snakes in Virginny if I don't do it!" Of flirtations or amorous adventures, he had absolutely none. In fact he seems to have had very little interest in women and to have avoided them as much as he could politely do so. Nor did he care much for cards or games, although one might think that they would have provided solace for his tired brain. He did enjoy conversation, and it was said that "his familiar talk was the best revelation of his genius." He kept in touch with everything that was going on in the world, and was ready to meet others on any topic.

Choate's handwriting, as those who have had to decipher his letters know only too well, was almost unique, being equaled in illegibility only by that of Horace Greeley. It has been described as resembling "the tracks of wildcats, with their claws dipped in ink, dashing over the folio surface of a sheet of white paper." His autograph looks, according to one observer, "like a piece of crayon sketching done in the dark with a three-pronged fork." His students used to study his notes as they would a dead language, like Greek or Hebrew. He was accustomed to boast that, if he ever failed to make a living at the Bar, he could go to China and earn a fortune by his pen,—that is, by decorating tea chests. When a judge once asked him to write out his argument, Choate answered in his dry way,—"I write well, your Honor, but *slowly*." His handwriting was an expression of his nervous, unreposeful personality.

He rarely laughed out loud, even at the most amusing incident, but he would throw his head back, drawing in his breath with a kind of deep sigh, while his eyes twinkled and his face glowed with fun. His wit pervaded everything he said. One could not talk with him two minutes without hearing some remark which was striking in its originality. When the qualifications of a certain officeholder were being discussed, Choate looked up and said, "You may sum him up by saying that he is self-sufficient, all-sufficient, and insufficient." As he was turning one morning into a narrow lane leading from Washington Street to the Court House in Boston, a friend greeted him. Choate looked around and said, with mock gravity, as he entered the alley, "Convenient,—but *ignominious!*" When Professor Webster, the murderer of Parkman, was in jail, he was visited now and then by a clergyman, who believed him to be innocent. "How do you find the subject of your pastoral care?" asked Choate of the reverend gentleman. "Well," was the jocose reply, "I always find him in."

[250]

"And," replied Choate with delightful ambiguity, "it will be long, I think, before you find him out." At a Commencement Day in Hanover, Choate was walking in a crowd, when a lady, passing him, caught a button of his coat in the knotted fringe of her shawl. As he turned to disentangle himself, he said, "Madam, I beg pardon; I should be delighted to go with you, but I have an engagement in the opposite direction."

He had a whimsical tendency to exaggeration which delighted his friends. Attending a performance of Mozart's *Don Giovanni* was like listening to "ten thousand forests of birds." When a Boston lawyer who was the very embodiment of all the conventional virtues was sitting in his office conferring with the equally respectable directors of a business corporation, Choate darted in impetuously and exclaimed, "Well, sir, I am glad to find you in your office for once. Do you know that for the past forty-eight hours I have hunted for you day and night through every theatre, bar-room, and dance-hall of the city of Boston without getting a sight of you?" The incongruity of this charge with the reputation of the lawyer, who was known as the most decorous and fastidious of men, set the directors in a gale of laughter. When Emory Washburn was late in meeting an appointment, he was welcomed by Choate with the

[251]

words, "I am glad you have come at last, for I have been waiting for you just fifty thousand years!"

In his conversation, Choate touched upon many topics, but never upon trivial or scurrilous gossip. He was ready to discuss with intelligence and fervor any subject dealing with philosophy, literature, jurisprudence, or history, and it was seldom that he did not have something very original to contribute. When he was aroused, his large eyes gleamed with his enthusiasm. A woman who had some reputation as a fortune teller came once to consult him. She had not proceeded far before she stopped and said, "Take them eyes off of me, Mr. Choate, or I can't go on." An old farmer who heard him in an eloquent moment, said, "Why, that fellow can cant his countenance so as to draw tears out of your eyes!"

At rare moments Choate would discuss religious problems, and what he said indicated that he had given them deep thought. From his early manhood he had been a fairly regular attendant at church, his preference being the Congregational denomination. He wrote his pastor from Washington, "The Sabbath bells do not a little bit aggravate home-sickness." Although he was not a communicant, he was undoubtedly a careful student of both the Old and New Testaments; but he would not allow himself to be interrogated on the

[252]

matter of his own personal creed. Prayers were said every morning in his house, as they had been in that of his and Mrs. Choate's parents, and there was always a brief "grace before meat," in the old New England fashion. He thanked an author for a book on "this grand, sad subject of the immortality of man," and, in a conversation with George W. Nesmith towards the end of his life, Choate is reported to have said, "My light here is soon to be extinguished. I think often of the grave. I am animated by the hope of that glorious immortality to be enjoyed in a kingdom where sin and sorrow cannot come." We have reason to believe that, as Brown says, "the faith of his father and mother were his to the last, and perhaps more decidedly at the last than ever before."

CHAPTER XII

Closing Days

*A*FTER the serious operation on his leg in 1855, Rufus Choate was only too well aware that his physical machinery was wearing out. One of his friends, noticing the condition of his health, urged him to go away for a rest, saying, "If you continue your professional labors without a vacation, you will certainly undermine your constitution." "Sir," responded Choate gravely, "the constitution was destroyed long ago; I am now living under the by-laws." He did not abandon his legal practice, making some of his most brilliant arguments in 1857 and 1858; but he grew tired very easily, and he no longer had that marvelous recuperative power which had sustained him in the past.

On March 10, 1858, he delivered a lecture on *Jefferson, Burr, and Hamilton*, in which he reviewed some of the fundamental ideas which had determined the nature of our government. On Independence Day in the same year he spoke in Tremont Temple, before the Boston Democratic Club, on *American Nationality*,

[254]

Some of Its Conditions and Some of Its Ethics, his real topic, however, being his favorite theme in those stormy days,—the preservation of the Union. During this, his last address on a subject of general political interest, his voice was so weak that it could barely be heard in the rear of that vast auditorium; but the earnestness of his manner lent solemnity to his utterance. Edward Everett, who was on the platform, said of the peroration,—"The charmed silence seemed for a while to prolong the charming strain, and it was some moments before I was willing to admit that the stops were closed and the keys hushed." This was indeed a generous tribute from one great orator to another.

In the summer of 1858 he was obliged regretfully to give up an engagement which he had made to speak at the Dartmouth Commencement, and instead sought recreation among his boyhood haunts at Essex. Perhaps, as he sat very quietly on the sunny slopes of Hog Island, he reviewed his career, from the time when he could first remember the crested billows breaking monotonously against the shore. He was not an old man,—not yet threescore,—but he had packed a great deal into a short period. Possibly recollections haunted him of that crowded church at Hanover in 1819, when he stood trembling as valedictorian before his classmates; of those expectant but discouraging early days in South Danvers,

[255]

when it seemed as if clients would never come; of some of his first successes before a jury, which had brought him the thrill of popular applause; of his experiences in Washington, as Congressman and Senator, and of the great statesmen among whom he had moved as an equal, —Webster and Clay and Calhoun and the others, most of whose voices were now silent forever; of intense moments in Faneuil Hall, when he had held audiences spellbound by the witchery of his language; of that late afternoon in 1853, when, once more in Hanover, this time as the most distinguished living graduate of the college, he had repaid richly the debt he owed to Daniel Webster; of troubled nights and stormy days, during which he never ceased to dread lest his beloved country might be riven asunder by the machinations of fanatics. Much had happened in the nation since little Rufus Choate used to paddle his home-made dugout down through the Ipswich marshes to the sea. The dreamy, studious boy had become a notable figure. . . . And we may be sure that there were intervals in his retrospection when his mind dwelt on the future and what it was to bring to the Union which he had joined with Webster in striving faithfully to preserve.

Throughout the ensuing winter, Choate seemed to be almost his old self, arguing several cases with a felicity of phrasing and a vehemence of manner which reminded people of his prime. He appeared on January 18, 1859, at the Revere House, at the celebration of the seventy-seventh anniversary of the birthday of Daniel Webster. His old Essex friend and rival, Caleb Cushing,—now, like himself, proscribed, and a member of the Democratic Party,—was Chairman, and introduced Choate in kindly words. Gaunt, and very weak, but struggling for his former energy, Choate delivered his closing sentences so that "the solemn-toned syllables sounded not like a speech, but a grand burial anthem." When he said sadly, "Oh, for an hour of Webster now!" he seemed like the Jeremiah of a passing generation.

At the twenty-fifth anniversary of the settlement of his pastor, Rev. Nehemiah Adams, Choate spoke, on March 28, before a considerable assemblage of clergymen and laymen, in praise of the creed which he held, saying, "We have attended this church, attached ourselves to this congregation, and adhere to this form of faith, because we believe it to be the old religion, the true religion, and the safest." On the following day he made his last argument before the full bench of the Supreme Court, the case being that of *Gage* v. *Tudor*. He still continued, however, to attend his office each morning, lying on his sofa while he advised his clients; and early in April he actually took a trip to Salem to appear in court in the matter of a contested will. His

[257]

last remarks before a judge were thus made in the city where his first successes had been gained. . . . Before this case was closed, he was obliged to withdraw and return to his home. For some months he had been troubled with a frequently recurring nausea and an enervating lassitude which he believed to be due to a heart ailment. We can now recognize that they were the symptoms of Bright's Disease, which might conceivably have been retarded if a proper diagnosis had been made and he had been willing to submit to a regular routine prescribed by a physician.

It was a blessing that he had around him a family to comfort his declining years. His two oldest children, as we have seen, died in infancy, but his third child, a daughter, Helen Olcott Choate, married Joseph Mills Bell, and, after her husband's death in 1868, lived on well into the twentieth century. A second daughter, Sarah Blake Choate, never married, but died in 1875, at the age of forty-four. Rufus, the only son, went to Amherst College,—why he did not attend Dartmouth I cannot ascertain,—and to Harvard Law School, and had begun the practice of his profession in Boston with every outlook for success, when the Civil War broke out. He joined the Second Massachusetts Regiment, fought in several engagements, and was promoted to a captaincy, but was then attacked by a malady which compelled him

[258]

to resign his commission. He died on January 16, 1866. Another daughter, Miriam Foster Choate, married, in 1856, Edward Ellerton Pratt, a Harvard graduate, a lawyer, and, for many years, Treasurer for the Boston District of the Chicago, Burlington & Quincy Railroad. Thus Rufus Choate had, besides his wife,—who was something of a chronic invalid,—one son and three daughters, two of whom had married young men whom he liked. Both of these, after their marriages, lived in Boston, close by, where they could visit him every day at his home.

Acting on the best medical advice available, Choate considered a voyage to Europe, planning to sail in the middle of May and spend the summer on the Isle of Wight; but when the day of embarkation arrived, he was too feeble to undertake such a journey, and instead, he moved from the city to the Bell residence in Dorchester, then a popular suburb of Boston. Freed reluctantly from the chains of his practice, he turned to his two solaces,—books and the sea,—the companions of his maturity as they had been of his youth. Early in the morning he read the *Bible*, as he always had done, and then glanced through the newspapers for the reports of court proceedings. Although he suffered no pain, he was so weak that it was impossible for him to walk the length of the yard without resting. Each after-

[259]

noon he drove with his daughter, sometimes back to Boston, past the Court House,—which he glanced at with longing eyes, as a disabled general might survey the battlefield where he had won his most famous victory,— but oftener to the beach, where he was content to lie on the sand for hours, his gaze directed towards the spreading sails in the harbor. The mind of the man was as alert as ever, and his courage was unfailing; but that much-abused and worn-out body was at last giving away.

The eminent specialists whom he consulted insisted that a summer in England might renew his strength, and so, although he himself was conscious that he was in the valley of the shadow, he proceeded with preparations for the voyage. From his library he chose certain book to be his companions: the *Bible;* some of the familiar classics, like Bacon, Shakspere, Milton, and Coleridge; Macaulay's *History of England;* Lewis's *Six Days of Creation;* the *Iliad;* and Luther's *On the Psalms.* They were not "light reading," but Rufus Choate lived before the days when weary statesmen reveled in detective stories. That he was doubtful whether he would ever return alive is clear from some references in his farewell letters. On June 29, he boarded the *Europe,* all his family accompanying him to his stateroom, where he at once lay down on the sofa, unwilling and unable to move farther. In view of what we know to-day about his disease, it seems criminal that he was allowed to sail at all.

His son, Rufus, accompanied him, and an old friend, George S. Hillard, happened by chance to be on the same boat. "From the moment I looked upon him, on the morning of the day we sailed," said Mr. Hillard, "I felt assured that the hand of death was on him." Hour after hour he lay inert in his cabin, suffering slightly from seasickness, but unwilling even to change his position. He seemed to be completely prostrated. On the second day his hands began to swell, and two physicians on board saw that his condition was so serious as to make it unwise for him to proceed beyond Halifax, where the *Europe* made her first stop. On June 30, at midnight, the vessel reached this port, and Rufus Choate, under the dim lamplight at the docks, staggered to a carriage, hardly able to stand. When the father and son arrived at the boarding house to which they had been recommended, the landlady told them that she had no unoccupied beds, and the younger Rufus had to wander about the strange city in the early hours of the morning, seeking shelter for the dying statesman. Somehow quarters were discovered, but Choate, too weak to ascend the stairs to the third story of the house, slept on a sofa in a lower room. On the next day he was carried up to some comfortable apartments, where he had a view of the harbor, and, from his bed, could, without raising himself from his pillow, watch the unloading at the wharves and the vessels getting under way. Faint memories of other times came flooding to his mind. "If a schooñer or a sloop goes by," he whispered to his son, "don't disturb me, but if there is a square-rigged vessel, wake me up."

The summer days passed one by one, while Rufus Choate lay helpless far from his home. The American Consul in Halifax was assiduous in his attentions. Occasionally, as he regained a little vitality, he talked of going back to Essex and having a boat built there in which he could explore the coast. His dreams were all of Hog Island and the Ipswich shore, every rod of which he had traversed. On July 12, he was apparently a little better, and sitting up in bed, ate a hearty dinner. Soon after he had finished, his son was startled by hearing him make some incoherent request, and rushed to his side. "I don't feel well; I feel faint," he muttered in a low tone. They were his last words. . . . Restoratives were administered, and the physician was summoned without delay, but Rufus Choate never regained consciousness. He continued to breathe, but very heavily, until twenty minutes of two on the following morning, when his heart quietly stopped. It was a peaceful ending for such a fiery soul.

As soon as the sad news reached Boston, on July 14, condolences began to roll in. On July 19, at a meeting of the Suffolk County Bar, Charles G. Loring presented a series of special resolutions for adoption, and Richard Henry Dana, Jr., gave a glowing eulogy of the dead orator. "In his presence," said Dana, using one of those glorious similes of which Choate himself was so fond, "I felt like the master of a small coasting vessel, that hugs the shore, that has run up under the lee to speak to a great homeward bound Indiaman, freighted with silks and precious stones, spices and costly fabrics, with sky-sails and studding-sails spread to the breeze, with the nation's flag at her mast-head, navigated by the mysterious science of the fixed stars, and not unprepared with weapons of defense, her decks peopled with men in strange costumes, speaking of strange climes and distant lands." Dana acted on an infallible instinct when he drew his figure from ships that sail the seas.

On Friday, July 22, Faneuil Hall flung open her doors at midday while a public meeting of the citizens of Boston was held to honor the Great American Advocate. He who had so often and so beautifully spoken the eulogy of others was now himself to receive merited praise. The pillars and galleries were draped in mourning, and the light of day was excluded, the hall being illuminated by gas. There were several speakers, but

[263]

the one most eagerly awaited was Choate's friend and political associate, Edward Everett, like him a founder of the Whig Party. Talking simply, but from the depths of his heart, Everett dwelt on Choate's noble qualities,—"If ever there was a truly disinterested patriot, Rufus Choate was that man. In his political career there was no shade of selfishness. . . . Our friend was, in all the personal relations of life, the most unselfish and disinterested of men. . . . He reaped little but fame, when he ought to have reaped both fame and fortune. . . . His work is done,—nobly, worthily, done. . . . To-morrow we shall follow him,—the true patriot,—the consummate jurist,—the eloquent orator, —the honored citizen,—the beloved friend,—to the last resting place; and who will not feel, as we lay him there, that a brighter genius and a warmer heart are not left among living men." It was a tribute which Edward Everett could speak with sincerity, for every word of it was true.

While this meeting was going on, the steamboat bringing the body of Rufus Choate came to anchor in Boston Harbor. On the next day a private funeral ceremony was held at the Choate home in Winthrop Place, with a public service afterwards in the Essex Street Church, attended by prominent officials of the city and the Commonwealth. There was an impressive funeral cortege which moved slowly through the main streets of the city. He was buried under the trees of Mount Auburn Cemetery, where a simple block of granite marking his resting place bears merely the words RUFUS CHOATE. When Somerby, the eminent Boston lawyer, was riding with a friend along the cemetery paths, he took off his hat at a certain spot with an air of reverence. His companion asked him what he was doing. "That," said Somerby, pointing to a stone at the top of a flight of steps, "is the grave of Rufus Choate. The man who goes by that grave without taking off his hat is not fit to live on earth."

CHAPTER XIII

An Attempt at Appraisal

*T*O the men and women of Rufus Choate's generation, who had seen that expressive countenance and listened to that persuasive voice, he was palpably a figure of importance,—perhaps Boston's foremost citizen. No one was more talked about than he, and his entrance at any public gathering was a signal for applause. Good stories were launched under cover of his name, just as *bon mots* now are attributed to Chauncey M. Depew. Even while he was still alive, he was the subject of serious analytical discussion by the scholarly Edwin P. Whipple in his *Essays and Reviews* and by Edward G. Parker, a student in Choate's office, in his *Golden Age of American Oratory*. Within a year after his death, Parker, who aspired to the rôle of Boswell, published his *Reminiscences of Rufus Choate*, badly arranged and carelessly written, but containing some useful material. In 1884, Joseph Neilson brought out his *Memories of Rufus Choate*, valuable chiefly because of the letters which it included from Choate's friends. Meanwhile,

[266]

in 1862, Professor Samuel Gilman Brown, of Dartmouth, afterwards President of Hamilton College, prepared, with the approval and assistance of Mrs. Choate,—who did not die until December 8, 1864,—two imposing volumes under the title *The Works of Rufus Choate with a Memoir of His Life,* comprising some of his best lectures and addresses. Because Brown was aided by Rufus Choate, Jr., and by Edward Ellerton Pratt, Esq., the book had the status of an authorized biography.

The various chroniclers of political gossip, like Sargent and Boutwell and Poore, have also had many incidents to relate of Rufus Choate.

Distinctions were bestowed upon Choate in abundance,—honorary degrees from universities, memberships in learned societies, and other complimentary decorations which fall to the lot of those who have achieved success. He was made Doctor of Laws by Yale in 1844, Dartmouth in 1845, Harvard in 1845, and Amherst in 1848.

And indeed no one can turn the fading pages of the Boston newspapers of the "40's" and "50's" without reaching the conclusion that Rufus Choate was then regarded as belonging among America's immortals. William Wetmore Story, who knew and loved him, could refer ecstatically to

[267]

the clustering hair
And flashing eyes of Choate, whose rare
Full-worded eloquence had power to thrill
And move and mold his hearers to his will.

Edward Everett, who seldom said more than he meant, stated that Choate stood "at the head of his profession in this country." Governor John H. Clifford assigned him "the first place among this generation of American lawyers." Enoch L. Fancher called him "the greatest lawyer and the most eloquent orator of his time." For further evidence, let me quote Senator George F. Hoar's well-known mention of "Rufus Choate, next to Webster himself the foremost forensic orator of modern times, against whose imperial eloquence no human understanding, either on the Bench or in the jury box, seemed to be proof." These are all matured opinions, by men of experience and sound judgment.

What shall we say of him now, after the lapse of three-quarters of a century? We must begin by admitting that his rank as a statesman is probably not so high to-day as it seemed to be in 1850. His sincerity of purpose, his undeviating patriotism, and his lofty standard of public morality set him apart from some of the venal and self-seeking politicians around him, and his very incorruptibility was in itself a distinction. Never-

[268]

theless it was unfortunate that he identified himself with no great constructive project, such as the annexation of Texas or the overthrow of negro slavery. His refusal to join the Republican Party in 1856 led to his being belittled by Republican historians,—and most United States history, until very recently, was written by Republicans. If he had lived through the Civil War, he would undubitably have supported Lincoln, like Everett, Cushing, and other New Englanders who disliked abolitionists as much as Choate did; yet he has been erroneously and scornfully dismissed as "a Northern man with Southern principles." Choate's terms as Congressman and Senator were so fragmentary and his legislative work was so half-hearted that he cannot be called a statesman of the first rank. His most important contribution was doubtless his effort after 1850 to save the Union from the attacks of men like William Lloyd Garrison on the one hand and men like John C. Calhoun and William L. Yancey on the other; but even for this he has probably been more blamed than praised.

In considering him as an orator, we are on less debatable ground. He does not suffer by comparison with the very greatest, and he has often been mentioned in the same breath with Demosthenes and Cicero, Burke and Fox, Webster and Wendell Phillips. If we are to judge by the effect which he produced on an audience, Rufus

[269]

Choate was one of the finest public speakers, not alone of his time, but of all time. Here too it must be confessed that Choate had no such splendid opportunity as that offered to Cicero in his denunciation of Verres or to Burke in his appeal for conciliation with the colonies. But his *Eulogy of Daniel Webster* is probably the noblest memorial oration ever spoken by human lips, and some of his other speeches which stir us as we read them in the lifeless type must have been irresistible as he delivered them from the platform. His fame as an orator is, I believe, secure.

Nor has his reputation as a lawyer suffered the slightest diminution. In any list of eminent American advocates he must be included, and his position among the leaders of his profession is as unquestioned as that of Hawthorne among novelists or Bulfinch among architects. There is no attorney about whom so many anecdotes are perennially related and concerning whom such an enduring tradition has been established. He is still set up as a model for aspiring barristers, and by lawyers themselves he is regarded as the master of them all.

The criticisms of Choate, so far as they have found expression in print, have been based on two principal charges. In an editorial in the Springfield *Republican* shortly after Choate's death in 1859, when even his political opponents were joining in the chorus of praise,

Samuel Bowles rather ungraciously struck a note of condemnation:

> We refer to what was notorious in the profession, to what in one form had passed into a by-word with the public,—his disregard of truth and justice in the undertaking and trial of causes. In assuming a suit or a defense, he never seemed to ask, "Is this right? does my client seek the ends of truth and justice?" Nor in the prosecution of cases did he ever seem to hesitate in the use of doubtful or dishonest means to secure the end.

These are severe words, and the biographer of Choate cannot altogether ignore them. It is clear that Choate was ready always to do his best for a client. According to his theory of the law,—and with his theory virtually every eminent attorney of his day would have concurred,—any defendant, no matter how degraded, was entitled to the best possible presentation of his case. In his early days in Danvers and Salem, Choate unquestionably took cases which later, in Boston, he would have refused; but that he ever used doubtful or dishonest methods cannot, I think, be proved. The almost unanimous testimony of his colleagues at the Boston Bar exonerated him from any such offense. That he refused to defend Professor Webster has been shown; that judges and lawyers believed the decision in the

Terrill Case to be justified is easily demonstrable. The layman, unacquainted with the technicalities of legal procedure, sometimes held, as Bowles did, another opinion. But his associates concurred in feeling that no one adhered more faithfully than he to the old motto, *Pro clientibus saepe; pro lege, pro republica semper.*

It has also been alleged, especially by the Honorable Eben F. Stone, in a lecture on *Choate, Cushing and Rantoul,* delivered before the members of the Essex County Bar on February 2, 1889, that Choate "lacked the moral robustness for a great crisis," that, "his nature was not highly moved by moral considerations," and that "he cringed before the magnificent tyranny of Clay." The last accusation has already been refuted and requires no answer. It is probably true that Choate "failed as a great Parliamentarian," mainly because he was interested primarily in other things; but I can see no evidence that he showed cowardice on any political issue. His opinions on such matters were formed after reflection, and sometimes after a real mental struggle. When he had formulated them, he stood by them. He approved of the Compromise of 1850 and of the Kansas-Nebraska Act and of the Dred Scott Decision because he desired first of all to preserve the Union if that could be done in any legitimate way. After his death, James Freeman Clarke preached a sermon and Wendell Phillips delivered an address denouncing him for his critical attitude towards abolitionists; and Sumner, once his friend, was estranged from him for the same reason. But there was no cowardice on Choate's part. Mistaken and deluded he may have been, but he was entirely honest in the views which he held. The easiest road would have been concurrence with his former friends in the Whig Party.

I prefer, as an estimate of Choate's manhood, to accept the judgment of Joseph Hodges Choate, who, in an address on October 15, 1898, at the unveiling of French's bronze statue of the Great Advocate in the Boston Court House, spoke particularly of "the character of the man,—pure, honest, delivered absolutely from the temptations of sordid and mercenary things, aspiring daily to what was higher and better, loathing all that was vulgar and of low repute, simple as a child, and tender and sympathetic as a woman." He concluded in ringing words, "Emerson most truly says that character is above intellect, and this man's character surpassed even his exalted intellect and, controlling all his great endowments, made the consummate beauty of his life." This is an analysis more in accord with the facts. Choate was certainly no perfect character, no flawless Arthur. He had his weaknesses and petty vanities and overmastering desires like other human beings. But his motives were unselfish, his life was clean, and his

[273]

ideals were high. Whenever he made blunders, he was ready to admit them; and he always had a good reason for taking a position. If he sinned, he sinned in the company of Edward Everett and Caleb Cushing and Daniel Webster; and there are some excellent men who prefer these statesmen to William Lloyd Garrison and the advocates of a "higher law."

There are those who have lamented that a man of his amazing talent could not have stamped upon our politics or our literature the abiding impression which those who knew him felt that he was capable of leaving. It is, of course, to be regretted that he left nothing behind him except some public addresses and a few fragmentary discussions of ephemeral topics,—not a book by which his genius could have been perpetuated. It might have been better for his ultimate fame if some of the long hours which he spent in arguing trivial causes could have been devoted to that *History of Greece* which he once contemplated. In order to gain an immediate victory in the courts, he deliberately sacrificed a chance for literary glory. . . . But there will always be a question as to how much permanent renown he could have won as an essayist or an historian. That glowing and rhetorical style which so dazzled his listeners might have seemed too florid for anything except an oration. I do not myself feel that Rufus

[274]

Choate, as a writer of prose, could ever have equaled Emerson or Lowell or Parkman. Among such literary men, he would have had to accept second place; whereas, among advocates, he had to yield to no competitors. His reputation was,—and is,—unquestioned.

It is probable that Rufus Choate, in any age and in any country, would have become a remarkable man. There was about him, as there was about Benjamin Franklin and Andrew Jackson and John Randolph and Roscoe Conkling and Theodore Roosevelt,—to select five very different Americans,—something picturesque, and therefore appealing. He did not slide easily in the grooves by which the energies of common mortals are guided; he plotted his own course, devised his own methods, and refused to be an echo or an imitation. He could throw a freshness over familiar topics and could revitalize worn-out themes. It was characteristic of him that he could speculate seriously as to the practicability of importing camels for transportation purposes in the sandy deserts of the American Southwest. In many respects, Choate was a typical New Englander, who, as a boy, had driven the cows to pasture and swung the scythe on July afternoons; but he would have been entirely at ease upon a camel. He was an Oriental Yankee, a quaint blend of the Arab and the Puritan!

Because of some elusive element in his personality,

[275]

everything that Choate did seemed romantic. His appearance, his manner, his language,—all were impressive, and differentiated him from those around him. The most ordinary action with him became a ceremony, and a simple gesture seemed inspired. You would be in a bare and cheerless courtroom, almost stupefied by the droning of pettifoggers. Choate arose and commenced to speak. Presto! You were in a changed world! It was as if a pile of unattractive debris had been suddenly kindled into a warm and alluring blaze.

By a paradox which can easily be explained, Choate, who was intellectually an aristocrat, was one of the most democratic of men. Like Lincoln, he understood the motives of the average American, and he really enjoyed plain people. After all, he had attended the village muster and sat through town meeting and been the idol of lyceum audiences. His speeches were sprinkled with homely imagery drawn from the fishing and farmer folk of Essex County. He fitted in with them far better than with the genteel hierarchy of Beacon Hill. He liked a chowder made from Ipswich clams more than all the elaborate French dishes on the Parker House bill-of-fare.

Choate had no time to waste on "the flesh pots of Egypt" or in the brilliant assemblies and gay dinners of Boston society. While more worldly souls were seeking relief from *ennui* at Nahant or among the White Mountains, he preferred the miniature cosmos of his office. Like many a reveler, he often heard the chimes at midnight, but it was always because he was intent on the printed page. In the diversions of the fashionable, he found nothing to criticize, for he himself was neither an ascetic or a prig, and he was too broadly human to "damn the sins he had no mind to." It was merely that, for him, there were other pursuits which offered a fuller compensation. After all, he had not time for everything. "What can a person do?" he asked, only a month before his death. "Life is not long enough!"

No matter how we define greatness, Rufus Choate must, I think, be placed among the great. There was in him something finer than that which he accomplished. He scattered his talents prodigally in a dozen directions, and he left behind him no one achievement which places him beside Jefferson or Webster or Lincoln. It is lamentable that his alert intellect, his poetic and heroic spirit, could not have been employed in some magnificent work for the benefit of mankind. . . . But, even with these slight reservations, we must grant him some of the noblest traits of mind and will, conjoined to produce what we vaguely, but approvingly, call character. It is, after all, something to have been a useful and patriotic statesman, an inspiring orator, and perhaps the

[277]

greatest of American advocates. A unique and romantic phenomenon in our history, he emerged inexplicably from prosaic surroundings, wielded for a brief space the magician's wand, and then vanished, as if some meteor had flashed across the heavens, leaving a marvelous afterglow.